MISSION: FAITHFUL

To Betsy –

My best vet
friend,

Love,

Noreen

MISSION: FAITHFUL

by

N. Kay Carlson

This book is a work of fiction. Characters and situations are products of the imagination, the underlying truths are not.

The book *Touching the Invisible* by Norman Grubb, mentioned in PART IV, is published by Christian Literature Crusade, Fort Washington, PA 19034.

All Bible references are taken from the King James Version, published by A. J. Holman Co., Philadelphia.

ISBN 0-9665487-2-8

Published by T. Carlson
2440 Eighth St.
Muskegon Hts., MI 49444

Printed by Dobb Printing of Muskegon, MI

To my husband Tom

encourager, editor, ever patient

ACKNOWLEDGMENTS

Thanking one's parents for all they have done is almost impossible, except for the love we can return them. In this book, I can thank mine, John and Mary Grimes, for taking me regularly to church and Sunday school at St. John's Lutheran Church, Fredericksburg PA, providing a background education and baseline for further learning.

I thank the Poets and Prosers writing group and the instructors at the Maranatha writing conferences for helping me improve my writing and this book. I could not have written it without them.

PART I

PUBLIC EYE

Dana Dushane temporarily lost her job as secretary at the Secretary of State, or SOS as she fondly called it. Dana's working status bent with the leanings of Michigan voters. In the most recent elections, anti-tax sentiments had determined the sway. It took only a few months for newly elected state legislators to make their cuts.

It was late spring in Lake City, a watery tourist town on the shores of Lake Michigan. The young woman took a job sure to keep her afloat: a waitress on a dining tour boat.

At least the people will give me ideas for characters in my stories, she thought.

Dana lasted one very queasy night. She forgot she got seasick.

Though her parents had often urged her to go to college to fulfill what they called her considerable potential, even in her late twenty's Dana was not able to focus her many interests. "How can I declare a major when I don't know what I want?" she had asked them and herself countless times. They always temporarily folded when she argued that being a secretary was a perfectly respectable career.

And just as often she tried to figure herself out. She had often hoped she would do something special with her life, but a clear-cut goal never crystallized. Her only clue to any direction had been a vague desire to write.

Though she enjoyed working on her stories at the

simple oak desk her mother gave her when she moved out on her own, the rent bill lying by the side diverted her attention. The apartment was small, but she liked living alone and did not want to ask her parents to move back with them though they lived in the same city.

She wasn't qualified for anything in the want ads, so she swallowed her pride and went back to the unemployment office. The official there was surprisingly sympathetic.

"Not much else out there right now," she said. "We'll give you a check, but you've got to keep looking. Here's a seasonal one, just came in. Like the waitress job, 'til the end of summer. Strange though, told us to send only one applicant at a time. Someone who can read. Willing to try?"

"I don't have anything else to do this afternoon."

Dana marched to the address. It was in a residential downtown area, a small frame home with shutters and clipped hedges, well-maintained with no sign or other indication of line of business.

Maybe I made a mistake, thought Dana. But, she considered her bank account and rang the bell.

A young Oriental woman came to the door. After Dana explained her purpose, the woman said, "Please wait here."

The reception area was the home's living room, simple but eye-pleasing Colonial style. Soon a large-boned man with greying beard approached.

"Hello. I am called Saber, and you just met Flame. Please come upstairs to my office."

Who would call their kids Saber or Flame? Dana wondered. She hoped these were not their real names, but why would they have a code?

Saber's office was lined with wooden bookshelves. An oriental rug covered the wooden floor.

Dana gave him a résumé.

He glanced at it as he rounded the end of his desk. "Oh, you worked at a government job," he remarked. "Thank you, Miss Dushane. Have a seat."

He sat and looked at her intently. "We are a concern which becomes involved in certain situations, including mediation," he continued. "We are not lawyers, not government, not illegal."

Dana watched Saber trying to decipher her appearance. She knew her coloring was unfathomable, deriving from a redheaded American Peace Corps father who brought back a Jamaican bride. Their contrasting features had blended well in Dana. Her rich brown hair lay in abundant waves crested by chestnut highlights. Her skin was lighter than her mother's mixed Spanish descent, but darker than her fair, sunburn-prone father.

"Are you married? Do you have children?" he asked her.

"No, ah, Mr. Saber."

"Just call me Saber. Would you work for us with very limited knowledge of what we do?"

"I guess that depends on the pay."

He went to his file and pulled out a hundred-dollar bill. "It's yours," he said. "Go and check it if you like."

"I don't need to check it," Dana said. Despite the odd situation, she trusted this man.

"If you complete the job, you will be paid a considerable bonus, besides the $500.00 for each week you work."

Dana couldn't help a visible reaction.

Saber smiled. "Do you have any ties here?"

"Ties?"

"Are you free to leave the country for a time?"

Leave the country? What was she getting herself into? Still, she could not resist following this through. Her father came to mind. He had loved his Peace Corp travels, and often told her, "See the world if you get the chance."

"Just how dangerous is the job?" she interjected.

"No more so than driving your car."

Considering how she drove, Dana figured she was in grave trouble.

"Yes, I guess I can leave the country," the woman uttered.

"You're hired," he said.

From the start, they asked Dana to thoroughly follow a large city daily newspaper and a weekly news magazine, both of her choice. She worked on getting into order her passport, shots, VISA card, and traveling gear.

Flame delivered private language classes in German, French and Italian, teaching phrases essential to travel. Must be Europe, Dana thought, but still no word on her specific destination or business there.

She worked diligently for the business-like Flame. However, she found the French pronunciations almost impossible and could sense her teacher's frustration.

"Good evening. Bohn-zhoor."

"Good evening. Bon jur," Dana ejected.

"No, no. The 'o' is like 'over.' The 'ou' is like 'soon,' and the 'j' is like 'zh.' Bohn-zhoor."

"Bone sure."

Flame's expression of hopelessness prompted Dana to apologize. "I'm sorry. I don't know why I have so much trouble with French."

"You seem to want to pronounce your vowels like Spanish."

The student reflected. "Even though the Spanish were driven from Jamaica long ago, my mother's ancestors were of mixed lineage with them. It was my favorite language in high school."

And to put off her lesson a little longer, Dana asked, "What's your favorite?"

Flame's eyes focused warmly on Dana's. "I have always liked to learn any language. It's like breaking a code to get to know the person who uses it. But my favorite language is one I've noticed only recently. I call it 'soul language.'"

"What's that?"

"It's the language we use about our own souls. Much of it is relating to our bodies and a certain physical, geometrical space. Things like, *lifting one's heart; being on edge; shifting gears; up-tight; depressed; turning the corner.* I accumulate a list of the phrases we use to express our soul, and it's getting pretty long."

Dana thought for a moment. "Aren't the words just describing everyday occurrences that we relate to?"

"The key is that we *do* relate. The inner self experiences something which we express in universal terms in order to communicate."

"I think I get it. Oh, I have one! How about *dense*?"

Flame laughed. "Pretty good. I'll add that to my list. But we don't have much time. Back to French."

The fickle Lake Michigan can be cold in July, but

this summer stayed unusually warm. Between language lessons and pouring over news weeklies, Dana gloriously basked at the beautiful white beaches and clear, slowly waving water. Inland, she climbed paths of yielding sand, her walking stick providing traction. The glaciers of the Ice Age had long ago pushed away topsoil from Lake City.

Many of her friends had gone on to college, career, other towns, families. Dana liked solitude, but lately the ache of loneliness pulled more cloyingly. She was glad to report to her work each day.

Her only clue to the identity of the agency came printed on the paychecks. It was an acronym: FISH.

Dana Dushane owned no pets or expensive items to worry about leaving. Saber requested she tell inquirers only that she was working as a private secretary. She told friends she was going to visit relatives. At 5:00 am one morning, the phone rang.

"This is Flame. You will be traveling today. Bring what you have prepared. Your code name will be 'Dawn.'"

Dana's heart pounded as Saber handed her the tickets. She expected him to give her other items, a briefcase or attaché, but her only other charge was the address of the hotel she would be staying.

"We've got a car to take you to the airport," said Saber. "Enjoy Geneva."

A dazed Dana landed at the Swiss airport many hours later. After exchanging some money, she tried her French on one of the taxi drivers. He looked at her as though she just landed from Mars, so she thrust the address of the hotel in his hand and prayed for the best. She hoped he was honest, because she had not much idea of what he was charging.   The young woman was glad she hadn't exchanged much money.

The receptionist at the hotel directed Dana to an old-fashioned, tidy room.   A tiny refrigerator held cheese and crackers, which she gobbled gratefully.   A note lay on the dresser.   It said, 'Dawn: Please be in your room at 10:00 am Geneva Time Wednesday morning.'   Day after tomorrow.

The young woman collapsed on the bed, but couldn't rest.   The city was beckoning and she had to explore.

Dana Dushane gawked like any tourist.   She saw the beautiful St. Peter's Cathedral, the European center for the United Nations, and CERN, world headquarters for nuclear research.

The mountains and incredible blue waters of Lake Geneva reminded her of a recent church service reading about the seventy elders of Exodus.   How did it go?   *They went up and saw the God of Israel, and there was under his feet like a paved work of sapphire stone, like the very heaven for clearness.*

Tuesday evening, Dana numbly returned to her hotel room.   She fell exhausted to the bed and slept for a long time.   When she finally awoke, it was already the next morning, 9 am.   After stumbling to the bathroom, she was dismayed to find no shower fixtures in the tub.   How do these Europeans wash their hair? she groused, and somehow managed to wet and rinse her shoulder-length locks.   She struggled to dry herself and don a bathrobe when a quiet knock sounded on the door.

Her heart leapt.   For the thousandth time the young

woman wondered what made her accept this job. Maybe I'll know now, she thought.

A slender man of about 45 years and medium height appeared before the doorway. He was attractive without strong features.

"So sorry to come at inconvenient time."

"No, it's OK, come in," Dana said. It was such a relief he spoke English, she hardly worried about being alone with him. Besides, he seemed so meek.

His accent sounded Asian Indian, yet his skin and brown hair were light. He moved a corner chair closer to the wall to make her feel more at ease. "It is imperative to meet in a private place," he almost apologized.

"It's OK," she asserted again. Did her voice sound as trembling as it felt?

"I am with FISH. My code name is Rod. I have business with a few factional leaders of a South American country, one in which many people are dying in civil discord." He relayed three names.

She listened breathlessly. So that's why she was told to read the papers. Dana knew the names he mentioned and had indeed seen pictures of them. One person was the deposed president, one the army general who led the coup, and the other a leader of a disruptive rebel group.

"We meet here secretly. The press could not be told because many people would not approve. This is one reason why you were not provided information."

Rod's clothes were a light weight crumpled cotton. He did not have the look or air of a diplomat, but could more convincingly have told her he was the hotel gardener.

"We need a witness, an American, from the street, so to speak, who doesn't know us, doesn't know me," he groped to explain. "I have a gift, you see."

Dana couldn't fathom what he was saying, but she tried. "Even the UN and US Secretary of State couldn't get them together. You want me to believe you have them here?"

"You decide on the truth."

"Where and when is this meeting?"

"This hotel, in a conference room, in half an hour."

"Half an hour?" Dana exploded. "Please leave and let me try to get ready!"

"Yes," he said deferentially, almost bowing as he moved to the door.

"There is no more we ask, except to please not talk with anyone before the meeting."

The woman heaved a sigh. What if he was lying and the people were fakes? Would she really be able to recognize them? How could this Rod get such hostile leaders into one room? Why won't they tell me who they are? Should she call the press?

Dana thought of a new minister friend she had met just a short time ago, Allen Moran. He worked at a homeless shelter and seemed be in close contact with God. If only he could counsel her now. She closed her eyes in prayer; God, I don't know what to do and I need your help. She hurriedly dressed and left for the meeting.

Dana trembled as she descended the stairs. She could hardly grasp the door's handle with her sweaty palms.

The converted ballroom retained its Old European grandeur, with crystal chandeliers and sconces, ceiling paintings and gilt-edged moldings. French Provincial tables and chairs filled most of the room. A long head table ran along one wall.

Immediately she recognized the three men whom

Rod named. She was already sure they were not fakes.

The tension was dense. Aides and bodyguards warily eyed each other. A tall, heavyset man in general's uniform sat at one end of the long table. She knew him to be the head of the army which recently toppled the president. At the other end of the table sat this same president, hunched toward a woman with whom he was speaking.

On the room's other side huddled another group: the rebel faction. The leader wore a dark beret and camouflage army outfit.

Rod leaned over a clergyman who sat in the middle of the conference table.

Dana strode to him and asked where to sit. He introduced her as Dawn to Father O'Brian, a short, bald man.

"How do you do?" he asked in a warm voice which sounded American. Before she could answer, he said "Rod has told me about you. I suppose this must be difficult..." he faded.

Rod said, "Please sit at one of the round tables nearer the exit. The aides will sit there also." He was more nervous than he had been in her room.

Dana was barely settled when Rod left the priest and seated himself at her table.

The young woman puzzled over his position. "Rod, I thought you'd be leading the session."

"It is not my purpose to be in the center of activities."

Father O'Brian called the meeting to order. Three people of each group, including their leaders, gathered at the long table.

"We will begin today with a prayer, as agreed

upon." The priest supplicated for a negotiation to end the fighting.

Fr. O'Brian continued with some general remarks. "It is good of you to come and meet with us here. It is of course our hope to see your people relieved from their suffering."

Dana looked at the leaders. The general and the president were closely following Fr. O'Brian's remarks. But the political rebel was fidgeting. He looked to the back of the room.

"Mr. President," Fr. O'Brian addressed the man to his right. He paused and a lieutenant of the rebel contingent from a table next to Dana's rose violently and shouted, "He is not our president! There will never be peace until my party is victorious!"

He drew out a gun hidden in a pocket and shot at the ex-president, who dove under the table. The bullet found its mark in a man approaching the intended victim.

Dana scrambled under her table, as did most of the rest of the gallery. She was too scared to breathe.

An anguished cry rose in the back of the room.

"No!" shouted the gunman. He had shot the rebel leader. The lieutenant was paralyzed by the turn of events long enough to allow Rod to leap powerfully across several chairs, creating enough surge to tackle the gunman. The rebel fell, weapon flying from his hand. It landed a few feet in front of Dana.

Dana felt her legs rubberize. Within a split second, she realized she had a choice. She may have only this moment to get out of the room, and that is what she strongly desired. Her other option was to go for the gun.

She sprinted forward against her own will and an oncoming rebel soldier. The lunging man was small, but substantially solid when their shoulders crashed. Her long fingers touched the barrel, and she wound them around the contoured metal. Her rival had reached the handle.

She yanked her hand toward herself as hard as she could. He had not expected such strength, and lost his grip. Dana grabbed the handle with her other hand and pointed at him.

"Stop!" she yelled in a voice she didn't recognize. She backed toward the wall, hoping no one had been able to get behind her. She made it, staying clear of the exit doors.

She now had everyone's attention, and hoped they couldn't guess her terror. She heard a man call "Emergency!" out in the hallway, then noticed Fr. O'Brian's absence. "Police! Ambulance!" he called.

Now Dana noticed the president's aide. She had also pulled a gun and pointed it toward the general and his aide, who watched her with obvious alarm.

Dana didn't know if she should threaten the woman. She didn't want anyone hurt, but hardly felt she was in enough control to tell an armed person what to do. Dana watched her nervously along with the rebel soldiers.

The president knelt over the fallen leader and announced that he was dead. A muffled wail rose from the one responsible, Rod still literally on top of his back.

It seemed like a century, but was probably less than 10 minutes. The man who shot the leader continued to sob. The aide held her gun, but made no movements. Finally, sounds from the hallway announced the arrival of police. Father O'Brian led them in.

The rebel gunman did not resist arrest. Rod spoke to the police in French and the others concurred with his story.

Dana and the president's aide gave their guns to a policeman. The officers took names of people in the room. As they moved around to speak with others present, the general shook his head and spoke to Rod.

"The guerrillas' second in command is jailed in Switzerland for killing his leader. Without question this will break apart their movement. It was to resist them that I took over the government."

A member of the military contingent was visibly shaken. He spoke slowly to the president.

"Your aide could have killed the general but she did not. We are grateful."

The leaders moved toward each other. They spoke in low tones as the ambulance attendants arrived and removed the body.

Dana watched the events with a numb detachment.

A press corp erupted on the scene. Visibly astonished by the presence of the famously hostile groups, they took pictures and asked questions of the milling aides.

After a few moments, the ex-president took over. "Gentlemen and ladies. Our country has been through great turmoil. Violence is never right, but neither are the structures which oppress the poor. My party is knowing slowly of its own part in unfair economic and social structures of our government. I will now move more quickly for change. The general and I were both reminded today of how short life on earth may be.

"I want to announce with great joy that I will run for the presidency of my country in elections taking place in six months. The general will have continuing talks with ethnic groups and allow more rights for all people."

The press surged toward him to learn more. Rod

was nowhere to be seen.

Dana feebly returned to her room, amazed she was not enraged. She immediately started packing, longing to be home and under her shower. A knock broke her daze. She opened to a grim Rod.

He started, "I am so sorry. We were wrong to bring in a witness... should have insisted more strongly...," Rod stopped and looked at Dana's right hand which still held the door handle. He smiled slightly. "And yet, perhaps God wanted especially you."

Dana dropped her hand, suddenly shaken by the events. She looked down, then back into his eyes. "How on earth did you bring these warring factions together?"

"It was not me."

"Then who?"

Rod's serenity returned. "The greatest Peace-maker of them all."

The story made the front page of the Geneva Daily paper, and received some fanfare at home. The press mentioned the involvement of Fr. O'Brian, but not Rod or herself. She was surprised reporters missed their parts in the scene, but realized the police had custody of the rebel by the time the press arrived. She was glad, because she wouldn't have known how to explain it anyway.

She took her last paycheck and the bonus from Saber in his office. She sat down at his request.

He paced the floor. "The name of this 'agency' is *Faith, Inspiration, Service & Hope*. It is funded by a wealthy entrepreneur who several years ago turned his life over to Jesus Christ. It consists of people from various disciplines and denominations.

"Flame's real name is Fuji Yamoto. As you know, she is a language specialist. I'm Eben Stroud, the administrator here. I have also studied theology and keep up my reading in it.

"We often use code names, since we are interested in protecting our privacy.

"Our members belong to their own churches from various denominations. We feel the Lord is richly blessing FISH. The group is unique as human individuals are unique in God's eyes."

He paused and took his seat behind the desk. He looked closely at Dana as he continued.

"The real name of Rod is Jares Ranjah. To give you a little background, Ranjah's father had built up a large export business in India after their independence. Mrs. Ranjah died soon after Jares was born and he was brought up in close relation to the children of Mr. Ranjah's American associates. They were taught Christianity, and Ranjah believes as we do. But he was also influenced by the Hindu ascetics of his city and learned deep meditation.

The Hindu ascetics are religious men who give up all material wealth, just as some Christians do. As a young man, Ranjah--he is called by his last name--decided on a similar lifestyle. He became known locally as a wise man and healer, and sometimes his prayers benefitted the ill, but not always. He told us he would get very perturbed when they didn't, as though only he, and not God, were responsible for the people."

He has told us his attitude changed from the early days. He knows it is God's great blessing to allow miracles to take place, and we all have them in our lives. But it is God who makes the final decision in a situation, and we accept when events do not necessarily change to our liking or timing."

Then Saber said, "And now, though I won't go into the details, Jares Ranjah seems to have matured into manifesting what St. Paul described as the gift of miracles. A few years ago he felt guided to come to America and found a home near the monastery north of Lake City. There he is free to attend services, and may use the chapel for contemplation. It was there he met one of our 'special agents' and became involved with FISH."

"Oh," Dana responded.

"Father O'Brian is an excellent mediator. He's negotiated successfully in several countries, but in this case was stymied. But, in this particular situation, our Lord was using another key.

"The wife of the general is a Christian. She remarked off-handedly in O'Brian's presence that a miracle would be the only solution to the situation. O'Brian knows our group and thought of Ranjah. He told the general and his wife about a man whom he believed has the gift of miracles.

"The priest secured a promise from the general to meet with the other factions if he could procure Ranjah. The general was the one with the power and had been the hold-out. Once he agreed, the others were willing to talk.

"Though we are sorry for the loss of life in this case, much more life will be saved in the long-run. Our plans are sometimes modified in unexpected ways, but this one was a doozy. We are sorry we didn't anticipate the danger we put you through. Our security measures were obviously lacking.

"The boss, this businessman who funds FISH, and some other members of this group wanted a witness because this was the biggest operation we've had so far.

We make efforts to stay out of the media now, but someday may want to publish our adventures. Like the verses in Psalms say, 'I will tell the world of the Lord's works.' We thought it would be helpful to have an unbiased viewpoint. Also, FISH operatives thought in the future we might have need for verification to possible sceptics."

Dana couldn't reply. She needed time to sort it out.

"I hope the bonus in your check will make up for the trauma."

"I'm sure it will be satisfactory," she said, getting up. "I must leave now."

Later, Dana asked Allen to meet her. She considered he might not believe her, but had to talk with someone. She invited him to a downtown hot dog joint, and explained her story was confidential.

"I'll be," he said after hearing it. "I heard some rumors about the group existing."

Dana was so glad he took her word. She said, "What I don't understand is..., never mind, I don't understand any of it."

He laughed and then took her hand. "You had a fabulous experience, Dana. God showed you these things for some reason. Hold them to your heart and let them teach you."

At the end of summer, one of the secretaries at the Secretary of State retired, and Dana was called back to work. Sometimes when Dana remembered, her trip seemed like a dream. But she kept the plane tickets and once in a while looked at them. She also read the Bible more and more.

Yes, she was learning.

PART II

THE SHELTER

In the drizzly grey parking lot of the nights-only shelter, several men huddled around a burning barrel. They stood in the city's transition block, between dilapidated homes and warehouses to the south and remodeled condos and shops to the north.

One man was about 50, greying temples offset by mahogany skin. He warmed his only hand and hummed a low, rhythmic sound.

Another was toothless and grizzled, shoulders re-formed in permanent hunch against inclemencies.

Several featureless faces watched the blaze from behind the inner circle. Removed yet further were some figures sitting on aged aluminum and vinyl chairs.

One sat a few feet from the rest. This man looked five years older than his actual twenty eight. His face, barely lit, emerged unmatched to the scene. Clean-shaveness alone was not that which set him apart. He would, in fact, stand out in any company. Serenity of countenance, the depth of gaze from his ocean-colored eyes, made him appear as one who had seen the afterlife itself.

The one-armed war veteran put words to the music:

Jesus, you rose from the dead,
  You are God Almighty.
Jesus, it was you who said,
  The low confound the mighty.

At the same time, Dana Dushane stood inside the shelter over a full sink of dirty supper dishes. She blew the hair from her face, hands completely immersed. Her visions of herself as a glamorous philanthropist had dissolved faster than the grease on the endless pots and pans.

Once again laid off as secretary from the Secretary of State office, the young woman was thankful of her bank account's sufficiency to supplement the unemployment checks for a while. She hoped, as they had promised, the current dismissal would be neither long nor permanent.

Dana heard people coming down the hall and peered over her shoulder as they walked by.

"Maybe we can push two twin beds together so the four Smith kids can sleep cross-wise," said the Assistant Director, Glen.

"Good idea," replied Pastor Allen Moran. "Let's go up and rearrange again."

Allen was at least part of the reason Dana had chosen this shelter to volunteer. Since meeting him a few months ago, she developed a definite fondness for the young minister. In fact, they had dated a few times.

For the past few months, he had been acting as the temporary director of the agency for homeless. On one of their dates Allen had told her his background. He had played outstanding baseball in high school and his western Michigan college. Upon graduation, he was drafted by a major league team with a hundred thousand dollar signing bonus. But after only a few months in the minors, he broke his ankle trying to catch a fly ball to the old stadium's brick outfield wall. Though the bone healed, the tendons were stretched and he never recovered his previous strength for fielding and running bases. That explained the slight limp

Dana noticed on a few occasions.

After four years in the same minor league team, he quit baseball. He felt he understood life's disappointments, and spent part of his bonus money to attend a seminary of a Protestant denomination to become a minister to the poor.

He returned to his home town but declined to head a church. He still had a little money left and wanted to spend time with Lake City's outcast and derelict. He often did so at the homeless shelter and when the shelter's director left, the board asked Allen to take interim directorship. Allen accepted with some reluctance. He didn't want to become a bureaucrat, but knew he would eventually need an income. Allen knew a few board members wanted him on full, but the others were looking for a professional social worker.

There he goes, Dana thought. She had seen Allen more on their few dates than she did here.

She was finally done with the dishes. At the same time she hung up her towel, a muscular arm appeared through the swinging door. Though Allen no longer played baseball, he stayed in good shape and now enjoyed other sports, including the upcoming cross-country skiing.

"Did Gilbert promise you a ride home?" Allen teased.

She glanced at the silver chain around Allen's neck, then looked directly into his forest green eyes. "You know very well you and Gilbert did." Gilbert was a pewter fish Allen wore as a medallion.

The nights were getting shorter and cooler. When they emerged from the shelter, dusk blended the shadows and sky.

The couple walked up to the men at the barrel.

"Won't be long before we're eating Thanksgiving

turkey," Allen assured.

"Al' right, Rev.," smiled the singer, Hayden Burns.

"I love turkey," the grizzly man cackled.

Suddenly, a dark figure ran from a corner of the alley adjoining the property. Dana saw something in his hand reflect the fire, and her quick cry warned the others.

Everyone turned. Marshall Curry, the man apart, was the target. He saw the person coming and fell sideways, pulling the chair on top of him.

The ski-masked attacker thrust a knife toward Marshall. He jumped away as Hayden and Allen reached the chair on the other side, and ran too quickly to be caught.

"Marshall," Hayden yelled.

"I'm OK. He hit the bottom of the seat."

Allen ran toward the building. "I'm calling the police."

Thirty minutes later, a cruiser rolled up. Allen tried to remember all cops are not alike. "The fans and the players have cleared the park, officer,"

"Just tell me the facts."

The witnesses corroborated on the descriptions. The policeman, older and overweight, nodded his head. He barely glanced at Marshall.

"We'll look into it."

When the car pulled away, the scruffy old man said, "No one care 'bout the homeless. You got to be dead first."

"Not even then," another insisted. "The paper never reported the one pulled out of the river."

A few days later, Dana had a day off from volunteering and was eating a leisurely dinner in her apartment.

The TV was tuned to the local station's evening news talk show, tonight featuring the mayor. The fall elections weren't that far away and politicians were popping into view more frequently. The format of the show was a mixture of the anchor-person host and call-in questions. The politician dressed impeccably. Her makeup looked professionally done.

"Mayor, you came from nowhere at the election, and managed to raise enough campaign money to be in the black the day you were sworn in. And now, you've developed some real estate which no one wanted, and it's value is going through the roof. Can you tell us your secret?"

"Under my term, the downtown has become a much more desirable place to live. I believe this foresight was more than luck. I've had a vision which is now unfolding. I knew the financing for the renovation of the old textile factory would be a major turning point for this city."

A phone rang on the set. "We have a caller."

The woman's voice came over a speaker system. "I'm from Walden Avenue. Many persons I know, and I myself, are concerned about the old shelter sitting right next to all our homes. It might've been all right when there was no temptation for these people, you understand."

The mayor responded, "We are going to reveal some plans quite soon for this building."

A pall covered Allen's office the next day when Dana delivered coffee. A few volunteers gathered to discuss the mayor's statement.

"They gonna try to move it to the edge of the city. After all the churches down here did to work with us," said

Glen.

"Not to mention transportation problems for these people to the health clinic and unemployment offices," Allen added.

"The biggest crimes are against these people. The gangs and drug pushers hit them hard."

Allen sighed. "The structure of this shelter is the same as the buildings converted to condos. Our renter is good to us, but the pressure to sell from local politicians would be too much for her. Not to mention the big profit."

They dispersed. The daily chores buried their worries temporarily. Dana pitched in to change bedding in the upstairs dorm and sort donated clothing.

Then it was on to supper duties. Once again the evening meal was done and Dana worked to clean up.

All of a sudden there was a commotion. One of the ladies screamed. Dana quickly dried her hands and ran to the main entrance. She saw Allen running down the steps. With his only arm, Hayden Burns was half-holding, half-dragging someone with blood-soaked jeans through the door.

"What on earth?" yelled Allen.

Hayden was out of breath. "Marshall's shot," he barely puffed out.

"Where did it happen?"

"Outside Kingsford Condominiums."

"You walked all the way from there?" Allen cried.

"After a couple blocks, a guy picked us up in his jeep." He turned around and pointed, but nothing was there. He looked down the street for an instant with a puzzled expression.

"Call the ambulance," Allen ordered Glen.

"NO!" shouted Hayden, returning immediately to

his charge. "It's not too bad--a grazing wound. I was a medic in the army."

Hayden turned and saw Dana. "Get some hot water--boil it first." He said to Allen, "I know you have some gauze and ointment." Hayden spoke clearly and with authority.

"OK," Allen said, relenting. He wanted the injured man to see a doctor, but wondered why Hayden resisted so adamantly. Did his withdrawn friend have a record? Or was it against their religious beliefs? The two men had been at the shelter for only a few days. Allen didn't know them very well.

They put Marshall on a couch with some towels. The bleeding had almost stopped. Allen collected gauze from one of the closets, and Dana came forward with a large steaming pot.

Hayden seemed to do a good job of wrapping the wound, despite his handicap. Marshall was conscious, but said very little. He set his jaw to the pain, and refused all offers of pills.

A few of the residents weakly suggested to call the police. "No police," said Marshall.

"Try to stay inside at night," Allen warned the group. "It's dangerous for anyone out there--you should all know that." The group started to disperse. Hayden and Marshall prepared to stay in the downstairs living center, and no one bothered them. The assistant director said to Allen, "Better go home and get some rest. Tomorrow is a new day."

Allen looked at Dana, "You, too. I'll drive you home. We'll get your car tomorrow."

In Allen's car, Dana said, "What are we going to do? Is this coincidence that Marshall was attacked twice? Is it random violence?"

Allen replied, "You know the fear of crime the residents of the condos and other rebuilt areas have about the shelter."

"I hardly think anyone would start picking them off from one of their windows."

"No, although maybe to scare them. Everyone has a gun nowadays."

Dana considered. "Maybe Marshall and Hayden are involved in crime."

"Hayden would be pretty easy for the police to find. And Marshall, I've never seen a face, an expression like his. Have you noticed?"

"Yes. He never says anything, but looks like he knows something."

"I think someone is after him."

Dana sighed. "I'd like to investigate but have no idea how to start."

"You start by praying," Allen smiled.

Early morning at the shelter found Marshall up and eating. He leaned on a crutch that had been donated for just such occasions.

Dana returned to kitchen duty. A teenager, Sheri, was there to help. Shelter residents were allowed to stay during the day if they helped with the chores.

Sheri's mother had cancer and could no longer afford both medication and rent. The 16-year-old pretended not to care. She smirked at others' smiles, and rebuffed any questions with sullen hums.

Her hair was frizzy from over-perming and dyeing, currently blond. She dressed with low necklines and high hemlines.

Dana was pleased when Sheri offered to dry the dishes. "Thanks," Dana said. "Everything quiet last night?"

"Um-hmm" Sheri answered, her quest for the higher shelves impeded by her small stature.

They had only started when they heard music coming from the living area. A folk guitar accompanied a full-toned voice.

Young one don't you know,
 You're living in the wrong land.
There's a place that's right for you,
 Just take the savior's hand.

The women put down their work and crept through the hallway in hope they would not disturb the singer. They turned the corner to see Marshall on the couch with an old guitar, another donation Dana recognized from its long repose in a corner of the shelter's thrift store.

Dana saw Sheri peer intently at the singer. The teen smiled for the first time since she had come to the shelter and swayed with the music.

The volunteer receptionist, Beth Carlisle, came from the opposite end of the room.

Marshall's dark brown hair was covered by a beat-up baseball cap. His nose was longish, straight and squarely shaped. His eyes were not slanted or round but level, above high cheekbones. Though not handsome, he appeared refined even in this setting. He now noticed the crowd and stopped abruptly.

"Don't stop," Sheri pleaded before she could check herself.

"What song is that?" asked Beth.

He smiled slightly.   "Just something I've been working on."

With more coaxing from the rest, he started to sing again. Dana and Beth sat down on another couch across the room from him.

"He's really good," Beth whispered. "I'm so glad I was able to come in today to hear him."

"Weren't you feeling well?" Dana asked.

"Nothing like that. It's just that my husband wants to have a party for our neighbors this weekend, and I've been so busy."

"Where do you live?"

"Kingsford Condominiums."

Dana was finishing the dishes when Allen entered the kitchen. Sheri was still listening to Marshall.

"Do you hear Marshall?" he asked Dana.

"Beautiful singer," she answered.   "I think Sheri's defenses have just been pierced."

Allen's brows rose beneath his slightly wavy blond hair. "Wonderful."

"Did you know you have a volunteer here from the Kingsford   Condominiums?   And she's inviting all her neighbors to a party. Imagine, suspects will lurk by the fistfuls."

Allen grabbed a granola bar from the cupboard. "Did you offer to cater?"

Dana laughed. "Now there's an idea. I could wash her dishes."

Allen munched his snack.   "Beth started as a receptionist and client intake worker about three months ago. I think her husband is in advertising."

"I'd hate to think Beth could have anything to do with the shooting."

"I know. She was very enthusiastic when she started, and a nice person, I think, but I've noticed some resentment from her against a few boarders here. Her husband's worked hard to get where he is. I think Beth feels some people here use the system by taking all they can get and therefore deserve their fate. It can be tough working with some of the poor. Some volunteers burn out pretty fast."

Dana reflected for a moment. Then she lit the water kettle and remarked, "Beth usually takes a tea break in the dining room about mid-morning. I think I'll do that myself today."

Dana went to Beth's desk. "Could I join you for break, Beth?"

"Sure. I'm about ready now."

They got their tea and sat opposite each other at one of the long tables. Dana told Beth a little about herself. Then she said, "Did you know Marshall was shot outside your complex last evening?"

Beth looked perplexed. "You know, I thought I heard something."

"Allen and I, that is, I was wondering," Dana swallowed and went on, "could we possibly come to your party? We are afraid there may be more danger for Marshall or other residents here."

"You really think it was someone from the condos?"

"The buildings are isolated on the small peninsula. They're well lit and regularly patrolled. It seems unlikely anyone would be loitering or openly dealing in anything illegal."

Beth looked embarrassed. "I understand how you feel. But Ed only wants to entertain those who can lead to business for him. Do you think we could, well, stretch the truth a little?"

"Kind of like taking on a disguise? Jacob disguised himself for his blessing from his father, didn't he?"

They nodded to each other with slightly sheepish grins.

The Kingsford Condos contained modern, pricey waterfront units of natural wood to blend with the sandy environment. Dana borrowed her parents' new car, in which the excited couple turned onto the private drive lined with beach grass. A swimming area sloped gradually on one side of the short, wide peninsula. It butted abruptly with the marina. The V-shaped buildings contained 5 large, multi-windowed units each.

Allen commented, "Hayden said they were just out for the scenery, but it does seem a little far for a walk."

Through one of the windows they could see brightly lit chandeliers and several guests gathered in small groups.

The condos overlooked Lake City's inland lake which emptied a few miles to the west into Lake Michigan. Allen viewed the layout. "The peninsula separates these buildings pretty well. There couldn't be much mistake about the source of the shooting."

"I can't believe how nervous I am," shuddered Dana. "I'm sorry I got us into this."

Allen grinned. "I enjoy the part of us playing a married couple."

Before Dana could react, Beth answered the door. "You both look absolutely glamorous!" she exclaimed.

It was true. Dana's long hair, the color of horse chestnuts, was drawn upward and clasped with a rhinestone barrette. Her turquoise blouse draped gracefully into a black silk skirt with folded velvet waist. Her tall, athletic frame gave a picture of nice proportion.

Allen had invested a year ago in a good Navy blazer. It looked custom-made on his muscular build.

Beth looked over her shoulder. "Ed!" she called.

He was walking from the kitchen. He scrutinized the strangers.

"Dear, this is Allen & Dana Moran," she explained. "They were looking at the condos the other day, so I thought I'd invite them to the party."

Ed's expression lifted. "Thinking of buying, are you? What kind of business are you in?"

Dana tensed. Allen was put right on the spot now.

Without hesitation, Allen responded, "Ed, I head a conglomerate. We're into a lot of different things-- furniture, clothes, food, housing."

Dana and Beth exchanged glances.

He's enjoying himself, Dana thought, after all the worrying I've done on his behalf.

Ed almost jumped from the floor. "I'm certainly glad you could come. Let me introduce you to the others." He led them to a group nearby.

Dana and Allen immediately recognized the tanned woman, trim and impeccably dressed.

"I'm sure you know Mayor Yvonne Taylor," Ed said proudly.

"Pleased to meet you," murmured Dana. The mayor's blond hair was styled elegantly. Her designer dress hugged her thin figure.

Also present was a large African-American man

with thick hair and eyebrows.

"And this is Perry Polk," Ed continued, "one of Lake City's outstanding CEO's. He owns a bunch of small hotels and motels throughout the country, not one of them alike."

"Glad to meet y'all."

Dana worried again. Ed might push for specifics about Allen's company. She knew he wouldn't be able to stay convincing if pressed. Fortunately, the host continued to the next person. "And this is Gerard Conrad, best lawyer in town."

More couples came through the door and Ed excused himself.

Allen said, "I hope we didn't interrupt."

Perry Polk smiled. "We were discussin' city bonds. The mayah has set this town on fiah."

The mayor looked very pleased.

Not one to waste any time, Allen said, "We really like it here, but we heard about a shooting which occurred the other night..."

The mayor's countenance changed. She looked around nervously. "Yes, I guess most of us at the Condos have heard by now. I spoke to the chief of police about the incident just today. He is increasing surveillance in this area, and I am sure you need not let this incident discourage you from buying. Even the best of cities have some undesirables."

Beth shuddered. "I don't like it that everyone has guns. I came here to get away from crime. But the people who live here have big cars and expensive jewelry. The more they have, the more worried they are about protecting it. And now someone is shot..."

Perry Polk laughed. "Down where I come from, a

little flesh wound wouldn't cause a blink."

The mayor stiffened. "Americans have every right to own what they desire if they work for it. It is the function of government to allow each of us to live in safety."

Dana steered back to their issue. "Do you think most of the condo owners here have guns?"

"Ah sure do," drawled Perry. "I'll bet the good lawyer does, too."

"As a matter of fact," he responded, "I do."

"So does Ed," Beth added.

"As mayor, I must protect myself from the unbalanced persons who might attack me simply because I'm a political figure."

Beth shook her head. "I think having a gun gives a person a different mentality. It's like believing you are no longer living in a good place. Perhaps that is naive. I don't mean to argue with my guests."

The mayor started citing statistics on the relative safety her efforts had provided for their town citizenry. Beth politely excused Allen, Dana and herself from the group. They clustered in the kitchen.

"The mayor sounds like a paid political announcement," whispered Dana.

"New companies don't come to high crime cities," Allen reminded them.

Beth spoke softly, "One of the guests told me Perry Polk is in trouble with the IRS. Something about contributing large amounts of money to a group he didn't identify."

The lawyer left the small circle and headed to the bar. Dana saw him through the open door and decided to join him.

"It was a good season in California last year," he laughed as he poured some white wine. "It's so nice out, let's sit on the balcony."

The scenery overlooked the well-lit marina, filled with large power and sailboats.

Mr. Conrad was quiet for several moments. Dana realized he was an attractive man. Tall, slender, with black hair well-styled in its natural curliness. His fine wale corduroy sport coat looked expensive, as did the rest of his well-matched outfit. He was in his early forties.

He finally revived saying, "Oh, I'm sorry. Corin, my daughter, is in some trouble, and it worries me. I'm afraid I'm not always good company."

"I'm sorry, Mr. Conrad."

"Call me Gerard, Mrs., uh..."

"Moran, but I prefer Dana."

"Do you believe statues cry?"

"What?"

"You know the stories you see on the news every so often. A drop of water on a church statue looks like a tear and people come flocking to it, who knows why. Or the village children of Medjugorje, in the former Yugoslavia, claiming they see and talk with the Virgin Mary."

"I've heard of them, but I don't know. I guess I never thought about it much."

"What if the opposite happens, too? What if an evil spirit, or angel, or whatever it would be, would appear to someone?"

Dana shuddered. "Awful."

"I'm sorry. This is a bizarre way to start an acquaintance. Let's change the subject. Where are you and your husband from?"

They nervously exchanged small talk as the

previous subject cast its unsettling echoes. But they relaxed after a time.

As the polite conversation was coming to an end, Dana felt compelled to say, "When I get upset or stressed, I like to turn on my favorite Christian music station. It calms me and reminds me Who is in charge."

"I haven't had much desire to hear music lately."

Dana rose and slid the screen door.   "Thanks, Gerard, for the talk."

"The thanks belong to you, Dana."

The next morning, Dana dragged herself to the shelter kitchen. They had left the party late.

She helped prepare the food and went to the dining room to serve.   Life is unfair, and so is nature, Dana thought.   Many walking through the line seemed either beaten and broken or unequipped for making their own way.   Then Marshall started singing again, a dinner prayer put to music as the others received their breakfast.   Her usual ache was sweetened by the serenity in his voice and dignity he imparted on the scene.   His deft fingers produced a smooth, soothing tone.

After breakfast dishes were done, Dana decided to approach Hayden.   He was alone in a storage area of the bargain store, sorting shoes.

"Hayden, excuse me for disturbing you."

"No problem."

"I can't help worrying since Marshall's been shot. Do you have any idea who did it or why?"

Hayden looked troubled.   He hesitated.   "Marshall's pretty private... I don't want to hurt him."

"I understand.   Don't say anything you think would

be wrong."

He glanced quickly at her and away again to his work. "I guess it's OK, some of it. Marshall's mother got divorced. His old man never gave them no money. She couldn't find no job that paid enough for her and the kids. They lived in a car for a while, then streets and shelters. She got hard and beat the boys some. Finally the children went to foster homes. Marshall lived in a few until he was old enough to be on his own.

"Hey, I was in a foreign war. A bomb killed my best friend and took off this arm. But Marshall had battles too. He could be fried by now--dead or addicted. But he ain't."

Hayden's direct gaze pierced Dana's heart. His expressive face flowed between wariness and wonder. "Demons can disguise theirselves. They can appear as angels of light. How would you tell bad from good, if one came to you?"

Dana stammered. "I, uh, don't know. I hope it never happens."

"It happens, Miz Dushane."

Dana didn't want to continue with this conversation. It uncomfortably reinforced Gerard's strange topic. But she was feeling frustrated.

"What are you saying Hayden? Someone is trying to kill Marshall. If the heavenly host appeared for dinner, I don't see where it would connect with this problem."

"Don' get upset, Miz. The Lord, He is good. He sees, He knows, He protects." Hayden turned back to his work.

"I'm sorry, Hayden. Thanks for your help."

Allen and Beth greeted Dana in the reception area. She asked them to join her in the kitchen, then told them of her encounter with Hayden.

"Strange," Allen pondered.

Dana turned on the kitchen radio.

Allen poured some coffee. "You know, I've been thinking about last night. Did you notice Perry Polk knew Marshall had a graze wound?"

"That's right," Dana perked up. "How would he know?"

Beth tensed. "Oh dear."

"What?" Allen asked.

"Well, I discussed Marshall's mishap with a few of the tenants during the party. I can't remember, but I may have mentioned his wounds." She looked sheepishly at each of them. "I'm sorry."

Allen drooped but was gracious. "You had a lot on your mind last evening."

Beth revived. "After you left, Perry came into the kitchen while I was working there alone. He asked me more about the shelter and Marshall. He wanted to know what the mens' schedules are like, and where they go during the day. I told him I wasn't concerned with those details."

"Anything else?"

"No, but you'll be the first I'll tell if I hear more," Beth said as she walked out.

Passing Beth on the way in was Sheri.

"Sheri!" Allen called. "I've really appreciated your work here."

The teen shrugged her shoulders.

Dana tried. "You seem to like music. Marshall's, anyway."

Sheri sighed. "I thought his voice sounded familiar, but I just couldn't place it."

Dana looked at Allen in surprise.

"Then it hit me. He sounds just like Louis Peters. But of course, it can't be him."

"Uh, no." The young director feebly tried to prolong the conversation.

Sheri looked at the plates in the cupboard and her mood broke. She pulled some off the shelf to set them for dinner. Allen and Dana exchanged exasperated glances.

Sheri placed the dishes on a tray and made one more comment. "It's so sad that Louis Peters left town." She pushed a cart full of trays out to the dining area.

"We have a new angle at this anyway," whispered Dana, encouraged. "Could Marshall be this singer trying to hide out here for some reason?"

"Wouldn't Sheri recognize him?"

"Maybe she just heard him. Maybe a local radio station played some of his music."

"Let's see what we can find out about Louis Peters."

The daily paper's librarian gave Dana a date on which a feature was done on Louis Peters. He also told her about another article. Dana went to the local library and got the microfilm to view. The feature had a picture of a man with long, wildly flighty hair, beard and dark glasses.

Aghast at the contrast between the picture and Marshall's demure features, Dana understood why Sheri wouldn't recognize him. The first article reported on the artist's schedule and freshly produced CD, being played on a local hard rock station.

The second article stated the singer was sought for abducting a minor, but believed to have fled to a northern area of the state.

The next morning Dana walked into Allen's office

before starting to work. She told him what she found. His bright smile disappeared momentarily.

"If indeed Louis Peters is disguising himself as Marshall, what on earth would he be doing here?" he reflected. His face failed to keep its serious look and changed to its previous optimism.

"You sure look chipper, considering."

"I just got a call from our Christian radio station. They're going to broadcast from here Saturday."

"How nice. What happens when they hear about our little attempted knifing incident?"

"They get the news--they know. They also know the mayor plans to move us. The management is sympathetic to us."

"What can they really do about it, though?"

Allen slumped a bit. "Not a lot, really. But they plan to do a few interviews, and at least get the thing out in the open."

Saturday was a crisp autumn day. The radio techs set up their remote equipment, a table with some chairs, and some colorful attention attractors. People from the street stopped occasionally to listen and watch.

The DJ, Sandy McNeil, came early to speak with Allen. They stood in the front entrance hall.

"These are some questions I'll be asking," the young woman said. Then she tilted her head. "What is that music I hear?"

Allen looked puzzled. "You're going to ask me what music you hear?"

"No, no, I mean now. Don't you hear someone singing?"

Allen listened. "Oh, that's Marshall, a resident here. He's the one who was attacked."

"He's just great--I'm one who knows. Let me talk with him." They walked to the sitting area.

"Marshall, I'm the DJ for WYWH. Hey, this is short notice, but how about doing your music over the air while we're here?"

The singer's brow furrowed. He didn't move or speak.

The DJ assured, "Hey, I know you've had your problems. We won't say a word."

Marshall Curry rose and followed them to the table outside.

"Hello, Radioland. We're broadcasting live from Lake City Shelter. We have reports the mayor will try to move the residents to a smaller, less equipped building on the city limits. She declined our request to interview her.

"We will be talking with Allen Moran, head of the shelter. But right now, I've got a treat. A resident of this place will sing for us."

Marshall moved his head and guitar to the two mikes which had been quickly set up for him. The full chords evoked from the simple guitar blended with the singer's rich voice. The tune was original.

Homeless and hopeless
  Often go hand in hand.
Jobless and aimless
  Wandering the land.

You can work for God
  Or work for a man
Men can let you down,
  But God has a plan.

After several more verses, he finished.

Sandy thanked him. "Just like the Lord to give us a treasure in an unexpected place. Hope you all enjoyed it. Now let's interview the director, Allen Moran."

Allen tried to be professional and factual. He spoke about fifteen minutes. The whole afternoon broadcast seemed to go well. The DJ thanked them all, then packed up and left.

Dana kept the station on for a while. She once again washed dishes.

Beth entered the kitchen. "How're things going?" she asked.

"The broadcast was great. What I'd like to know next is when the dishwasher is going to get fixed."

Beth smiled. "Those things cost pretty much. I think there's a special fund for it."

"I'll make a donation as soon as my hands unwrinkle. Beth, do you know Gerard Edward's daughter, Corin, very well?"

"A little. She seemed pretty straight-laced until about a month before she..."

"I know she ran away."

"She started looking different, I hate to say it, but sleazy. Instead of wool plaid, she'd wear thin colored slips. She told me it was what her new boyfriend liked. Corin became curious about the supernatural. She asked me if I believed in visitations--like the one in Medjugorje by the Virgin Mary, and other places where people claimed they saw her."

Beth dried a few dishes as she talked. "I said I thought it provided inspiration to some people, but you can't believe all of it. The mind does funny things, and you have to be careful. I think that young man she started seeing affected her. He was a rock singer, pretty crazy looking."

"The whole thing must be breaking Gerard's heart."

"He's having a tough time." Then Beth commented, "You know, I was a little disappointed in Gerard for jumping in with the mayor to grab up this building."

"He didn't talk her into it, did he?"

"No, but he didn't do anything to stop it, as far as I can tell. He seemed pretty cooperative when they were here to look at it."

"Gerard and the mayor were here to look at the building?"

"Yes. They didn't come in, but I saw them in the car."

"When was that?"

"A little while back, let me think. It was a few days before Marshall was attacked."

Beth put back the towel and left. A DJ from WYWH was on the air. He started reporting the large number of calls their station was getting. People were supporting the shelter. They wanted to know what they could do. And most of all, they requested to hear the singer again.

Monday morning came quickly. Dana brought Allen a cup of tea and the morning paper.

At the same time, Gerard Conrad knocked on Allen's door. "The receptionist told me you would be..."

He saw to whom he was speaking. "Mr. Moran, I wasn't expecting to see you behind the desk here."

Embarrassed, Allen started, "Uh, Mr. Conrad, I can explain. I'm afraid we were not totally forthcoming at the party."

The lawyer studied him a moment. "Well, it doesn't matter. I have some papers here for you to read and sign. We are claiming Eminent Domain."

He leaned over his briefcase. "Hello, Mrs. Moran."

Dana blushed. "I must confess also, Mr. Conrad. I am actually Miss Dushane. Please excuse me, I must get back to the kitchen." She dashed out of the office.

A few minutes later, Mr. Conrad appeared at the kitchen door. "Miss Dushane, could I speak with you in private?"

"There's no one here now. I'm glad to have this chance to apologize."

"Don't be concerned. I'm actually glad. I am sorry myself about this unpleasantness concerning the shelter. I wanted to ask you if you are free Friday evening and would be interested in accompanying me to dinner."

Flabbergasted, Dana at first declined. Then, thinking about possible inside information, she said, "Friday evening? I guess I can make it at that."

Dana hadn't told Allen about the date. He was upset enough, and she felt guilty. Besides, Allen would be worried, but Dana didn't think Gerard posed any danger to her.

Gerard escorted the young woman in his late model sports car to an expensive restaurant on the lake. Dana was glad her mother had just bought her a new dress. She could tell the lawyer was pleased to be seen with her.

"I'm so glad you came, Dana. You are the first person I've been interested in since my divorce two years ago."

"It's nice to get to know you, Gerard. To be truthful, I don't have any friends who are lawyers."

"A lot of people dislike us. We are in the middle of many pugnacious situations."

"Yes, I imagine. But can you completely separate yourself from the people you represent? You are paid by them to use your talents for their gain."

Gerard's expression changed slightly. "We care more than you might believe."

The waitress interrupted their conversation. When she left, Dana changed the subject.

"Have you listened to any music stations yet?"

"As a matter of fact, I heard the shelter was going to be featured on WYWH, so I tuned in."

"You did? You do care about the shelter, don't you?"

Gerard looked uncomfortable. "The music was OK--a little modern for my classical tastes. But I've liked folk music since college days. That live singer--I have to say he was quite good."

The appetizers were served.

Gerard took Dana to an active downtown hotel lounge. It had a dance floor and band. The music was soft enough to converse. Gerard ordered some wine. They danced a few songs. He moved his tall, slim frame gracefully.

"Gerard, why didn't you want to hear music when I suggested it to you at the party?"

He sighed. "Corin is involved with a local singer. She met him at a political rally. She's under his control, which makes me just sick."

"I am sorry," Dana murmured sincerely.

"Corin is very insecure. She wants support

constantly. I couldn't supply enough. She thought she could gain prestige by the company she kept. This guy fits the bill. He's a local celebrity and even claims some mystical powers. His name is Louis Peters."

Amazed at the connection, Dana prayed, Thanks God--You must want me in on this case. She said, "Please go on, Gerard. This is what you were talking about when we first met."

"Yes. He told her an angel was favoring him with news of future events. That he could know what was going to happen before it did. He told us to buy some stocks. I wanted no part, but she used some of her own money. They shot up in the next few weeks. When he told her to sell, they were up $20.00 a share.

"Well, of course she was totally immersed. The potential for power and wealth would be almost infinite. He seems to have a magnetic pull on her, I guess with all this mystical talk."

They listened to the music.

Then Dana asked, "Did Peters ever tell your daughter if the angel wanted anything back from him?"

Gerard shook his head. "I couldn't talk much about it with her. I exploded at the thought of it. It was after one of our fights they left, and I haven't seen them since."

"What did Louis look like?"

"Oh, he was about 6 feet tall, average build. Dark brown hair, but his hair and beard were so full I could hardly see his face, and cared less to try."

"This is all very interesting, but I'm afraid I'm wearing out."

"It's late. I've had a nice time, Dana."

"Thank you. So have I."

The next evening, Dana convinced Allen that helping wash dishes was good for the character. The Shelter board had presented a program to the residents earlier, and it was now about 11 p.m. The long, quiet halls of the shelter could be overwhelming even for the bravest. The residents were already in bed.

Dana was drying one of the last pans when Marshall pressed through the swinging door. His face was pale, his voice husky. "Miss Dushane, please..."

"What is it?" Allen asked protectively.

"Miss Dushane, don't go home tonight. You'll be hurt. Something will happen."

Dana retreated. She was more afraid of Marshall than his warning.

Allen took Marshall firmly by the shoulder. "OK, thank you Marshall. We know you are concerned for Miss Dushane's safety."

"Please," he repeated, but did not resist. They left the kitchen and for what seemed ages Dana was alone.

Finally Allen returned. He embraced her and said, "You'll be OK."

Dana still felt her legs shaking. "I don't like this one bit. Louis Peters has an angel telling him about future events, and now Marshall is making predictions."

"What about Louis Peters?"

Dana's emotion changed amazingly fast from fright to chagrin. "Oh, I spent some time with Gerard Conrad. I found out some information."

"You spent some time with Gerard Conrad? Since he was here to have me sign papers handing the shelter over to the city?"

"I'm sorry. I just couldn't turn down his invitation."

Allen chilled. "Oh, he's giving you invitations, is he? Dana, he could possibly be attempting murder."

"Well, maybe it was dumb, but he was a perfect gentleman to me. I know he's aiding the mayor, but we weren't exactly fair with him, were we? Anyway, let's not argue. He said Louis Peters told his daughter he was given some power by an angel to predict the future."

Allen still seemed upset about her date. Finally he said, "I can't keep my residents locked up. Marshall himself may cause you trouble if you go home. Of course, you can't stay here either."

"I'll go to my mom and dad. Please take me to my car."

Dana drove to her parents' home and let herself in. They were still up. She tried to explain things without letting too much out. They had a midnight breakfast, then went to sleep.

In the morning, Dana drove toward her apartment. From the main street she saw a few pieces of broken glass in the driveway, so parked in front. When she walked around the corner of her building to the parking lot, she was shocked. Five of the resident's cars were smashed, and two apartment windows completely gone. She noticed some blood on the blacktop. Another renter surveyed the damage.

"What happened?" At his strange expression she added, "I wasn't here last night."

"A gang fight. About 40 teenagers--guns, clubs, knives. Around midnight. A couple of people were hurt before the police got here. Some drug deal gone bad, probably."

Midnight. The time she got to her mom's. The time she would have driven around the back of the building and into big trouble.

The phone rang when she got out of the shower. Allen was strained.

"Thank you, Lord," he breathed when she answered. "I heard the news. If Marshall hadn't warned you..."

Dana responded, "I'm OK physically, but I'm not sure about mentally. I feel suspended in something scary. What's going on?"

"I don't know, but it's even more important to find out now. We're working on two levels -- one physical and one spiritual."

Dana dragged herself in that morning. She felt emotionally drained. She drank several cups of coffee, knowing they wouldn't help, but lacking the will power to resist. She and Allen sat at one of the dining tables which served as a break table between meals. They didn't have much to say.

"Hey, friend, why you just setting there? I don't have all kinds of time like you do."

"Well, look who the Lord just led in! Elder Foster," Allen beamed happily. "What, no juvenile delinquent to pull by the ear today?"

Elder Foster was of African heritage, with a face slightly scrunched but cute, about 45 years old. He spoke in a quick, cheery falsetto, unmatched to his big build. "And who is this pretty young lady?"

"This is Dana Dushane, a friend of mine." To Dana he said, "Elder Foster's a great guy. Works with kids in trouble."

"Happy to meet you. Just came to check up on my last case."

"Oh, he's doing great. Got a job, and he'll be out of here soon."

Dana ran to get him some coffee. Elder Foster sat down and happily told them about his new computer.

"Well, I'm glad you got a good deal," Allen said sincerely. "You know, I think you're just the person we need. I know you're short on time, but I'd like to ask you a favor concerning your access to police files."

"I have time for the Rev."

Allen laughed. "You can say no, especially if you don't think it's right to do. You and I have known each other pretty long, and I'd like to tell you what's going on. And with all your connections, maybe you can get some info."

Elder Foster listened closely. "I'll get what I can."

"Thanks a lot," Allen said. "That will be worth a lunch out, on me."

Later in the afternoon, Dana saw Marshall walk alone through the front hall, early for dinner. The shelter was so quiet and empty, her call to him almost echoed.

"Marshall, would you mind talking with me? Allen's out at a meeting. Let's go into his office."

When they were both inside, she closed the door and sat behind the desk. Marshall sat in an opposite chair. Dana sensed an uncommon dignity in this man. Though the facts piled against him, he evoked her hopes for triumph over adversity.

She started, "You deserve to know that you probably saved me from getting hurt or worse last night. There was a disturbance at my own apartments, but I stayed with my folks."

The slight change in his countenance moved toward a frown.

"I don't really know how to thank you. Is there anything I can do for you?"

"No. I'm glad you're all right."

"You don't have to tell me, but how did you know?"

At this direct question, Marshall could not contain a grimace. He took several deep breaths and sat silent for a few moments.

"You see, Miss Dushane, something, someone told me."

"What? Who?"

Again, silence.

"For some reason, several people I've talked with lately have mentioned angels," Dana prodded.

He looked surprised and for a moment relieved. He breathed out, "An angel told me."

So there it is, thought Dana. Now what?

"Marshall, do you know anything about your attackers?"

"No."

"Did the angel warn you about your own danger?"

"No."

"What else did this angel tell you?"

The interrogated paused once more.

"How about telling me what he looked like?"

"Oh, about 6 foot 2, wings, combat fatigues and boots."

"Army fatigues?"

"Yeah, green, but not olive. More like light lime."

Elbows on the desk, Dana pressed toward him. "You understand, don't you, that your story is pretty hard to believe."

"Yes."

"We know of a man who kidnapped, or at least ran

away with, a minor. This girl is still missing. The man claimed an angel shared its foresight with him."

Marshall Curry spoke calmly. "Julian, the one who appeared to me, said another angel, a bad one, is disguising himself to mislead humans in this city. But that was all. No details."

"Marshall, have you ever used another name?"

He winced. "No."

"Like Louis Peters?"

"No."

Suddenly the door swung open. Allen jumped in surprise.

Dana sat back, realizing how intensely she was questioning Marshall.

"Excuse us, Allen. You can have your office. I think Marshall and I are done."

Curry quietly rose and slipped out the door. Allen sat in the chair he vacated, since Dana made no move to leave.

"What happened?"

"Marshall and I had a non-talk." She told him the sparse details.

"The radio station called me this morning. They want Marshall to tape a few songs. They plan to promote him."

"Great, we boost a kidnapper to national prominence."

"Do you really think he is Peters?"

"Are you saying you believe all this?"

"What if it's true? Angels have appeared on earth many times."

"Yeah, two to four thousand years ago."

"Many people today believe angels have helped

them. You don't have to look far to find written accounts."

Dana shook her head. "If he isn't lying..."

"We'd be criminal to impede him. He'll never get another chance like this."

"You're right. But if Louis Peters is conning us for some reason, we'll look pretty foolish if he's exposed. I can see the headlines, 'Kidnapper Uses Shelter for Hideout.' For one thing, the shelter would lose it's support."

"Speaking of our cause, the radio is organizing a protest at city hall, tomorrow."

"Let's see if Elder Foster has found anything."

Allen and Dana walked the five blocks to the Valley Church. The older building was open and rambling with well-worn wooden floors. They slipped into the small office from which the Church Elder worked.

"Elder Foster!" Allen greeted. "What's the word?"

"I got a few words for you, friend."

"I knew you were the one to ask."

"You wanted to find out about that man at your party--Perry Polk. Turns out he spent a little time behind the bars."

"What?" Allen and Dana exchanged glances.

"About fifteen years ago. For unfair business practices. Co-conspirator to fraud. Took money and gifts from some bad dudes."

"How did you find out?"

"It's easy to get the name of anybody that served time. Once you know that, it helps to have a few friends in the police department."

"Anything on the IRS?"

"That's a little different. They keep those things pretty tight."

Dana and Allen tried to take it all in.

"Now, as for your friend Louis Peters. He's not as easy as you'd think. A lot of people saw him around--he sang in the bars here. But they didn't know him well enough to tell me anything. They don't even know how he looks because he always used the dark glasses."

"But I finally tracked a lady through the phone lines who he spent some time with. She said he started bragging about knowing the future. Then he met a city councilwoman who apparently took him seriously. He advised her on investments and she did pretty well. She decided to run for mayor. He helped her with the campaign, and she wo 1."

"Mayor Taylor?" Allen exclaimed more than asked.

"The same. Peter's friend said she would never've made it if it weren't for him."

"Could this source of yours identify him?"

"There would be a big complication. She now lives on the coast."

On the way back to the shelter, Allen and Dana sorted through the new information.

"I feel more lost than before we came here," Dana said dejectedly. "Why would Perry Polk care about some shelter dweller? He served his time, so it's not like someone could hold something over him."

"Unless he's done something else."

"But wouldn't Marshall press charges if he knew Polk was after him? It would be pretty hard to blackmail someone who was openly trying to kill you."

"Maybe it's not Perry Polk. Maybe Gerard knows Marshall is Louis Peters."

"If Louis Peters is some kind of assistant to the mayor, why would he be at the shelter? His singing is rallying people behind the shelter, and he wouldn't want to expose himself as a kidnapper just to bring it down, unless he plans to run and leave some note behind. It seems he'd rather stay and enjoy the mayor's success." Dana barely finished her sentence before gasping. "Unless..."

"What?" asked Allen.

She hesitated, then said, "Maybe he's planning to build publicity and then...I can't say it."

"Hurt or kill one of us? And still plan to vanish? The thought occurred to me, but I didn't want to alarm you. The mayor may be willing to give him big bucks to stay away."

Dana strolled quietly for some time, then eventually stirred. "I just can't believe it's Gerard."

"I don't know why you defend him. You hardly know him."

"I'll be getting to know him better. He called me again, and we're going out this weekend."

"Oh, fine. I guess my feelings don't count."

"Allen, I have feelings too. You haven't exactly knocked down my door lately. If you're not going to ask me out, why should you have any say in who I see?"

Allen's grip tightened on a daily paper he had picked up. "You know I've been very busy with the shelter's temporary directorship. Can't you wait until I am back on my regular routine?"

"Well, for one thing, you never asked me. For another, I'm attracted to Gerard. And I believe that is mutual."

"Dana, sexual attraction is not the only, or even best, factor in developing a relationship."

"Please don't preach to me."

"Hey, I'm a preacher. The only way to choose your mate for life is to marry the person God wants for you."

"And how, exactly, does God let you know?"

"That's the awesome thing. If you turn your mind toward Him, if you give yourself to Him, if you walk in His ways, He will guide you."

Early the next morning, a Friday, a small crowd gathered around the 3-story city hall. They lifted their signs with cries against greed and callousness. Gerard walked into the mayor's second floor office. The blinds had been drawn.

Mayor Taylor sat behind her streamlined black desk. Her usual self-assured demeanor showed a hint of strain. "Did you get the shelter's director to sign?"

"You know he won't until he and the board check all their legal options."

"What about the owner? She assured us she would be cooperative."

"She's got three years left in her lease. She won't sign until she sees what they're going to do. For that matter, they've got a pretty good case. Eminent Domain is more properly used for obtaining land for highways or airports."

"We've got to get that building! It's all part of the plan!"

"Calm down. You've done so well already, I don't see how the shelter would make that much difference."

"Sure, the downtown is more valuable now. But we still can't compete with other cities for the big stakes. I've got it on good authority that the Japanese will be looking right in Lake City for a location for a gene-research lab and hospital complex. If we'd get that, this town would be on the international map."

Gerard walked to the window and lifted a slat. The crowd continued its march. "What about the homeless?"

"If that complex moves in here, all the people will thank me. We'll have more jobs, more taxes, more donations."

"And a governorship for you? Or is it Washington you're after?"

Mayor Taylor first glared at her lawyer, but then smiled. "They will thank me."

Dana and Gerard attended a theater performance. Afterwards, they went to a quiet, cozy restaurant close by. They each ordered a small meal and glass of wine.

"Thanks, Gerard, for taking me to the play. I love mysteries."

"I do, too, unless they are my own."

"I'm sorry. It must be very difficult for you."

"Some times are worse than others. I think of all the mistakes I made."

"Certainly you can't blame yourself for Peter's influence on Corin."

"I realize I can't control people, nor should I even try. But I should have been more aware of Corin's problems."

"Even that can be hard."

"I guess I spoiled her. My wife and I were very active people. We made up for our absence in the wrong way, giving her whatever she wanted. For a while, she was the perfect daughter and student. As she got older, she became rebellious but still wanted to be the center of attention. Peters was like some of the youth of the 60's. He was unconventional, yet I think truly interested in politics."

"Peters was a VIP with the mayor before he left, wasn't he?"

"A regular Rasputin. He was after something, but I'm not sure what it was. He couldn't have had any public role, considering his un-barbered appearance."

"Wasn't Rasputin a self-proclaimed religious monk who tried to influence the Russian royal family over affairs of state?"

"Yes, more for prestige than money."

"If I remember, Rasputin had an uncanny effect on women."

"They fell into his spell."

Their meals came, and their conversation drifted to other topics.

At the end of the evening, Gerard brought Dana to her apartment door. He kissed her lightly. "Thanks, Dana, for helping me through a bad time."

The very next day, Allen invited Dana out to dinner. When it rains it pours, she thought.

Saturday evening, Dana climbed into Allen's car.

"It's so nice to have you all to myself," Dana sighed.

"How about a relaxing meal on the waterfront?"

"I'd love it. Let's go to Sandy Lake Inn."

The straight city road became more woodsy and twisting. As Allen drove, Dana took in the greening scenery. She revealed her new insights.

"Gerard compared Peters to Rasputin?" Allen mused. "You know what happened to him?"

"Rasputin? What?"

"He was murdered."

"Allen, I can't believe Gerard is a murderer. And if you do, that means you think Marshall is Louis Peters."

"I don't know what to think. You have to admit it's

funny Conrad didn't take a better look at someone who was badly influencing his daughter. I care about you, Dana, and worry about your safety. I have to admit I'm also fighting jealousy. I think the money he so openly displays could be affecting your judgment."

"I am not attracted by money," Dana objected.

"It happens more easily than you think. Beautiful condo, nice car, big boat, theater, fine dining. Don't they fill those beautiful hazel eyes of yours?"

Dana ignored the compliment. She was angry to be called materialistic, but had to admit there was a part of her which liked the luxury.

Allen was unstoppable now. "Used to be we took for granted that professionals and businessmen deserved large salaries and all these things. But now, after working in the shelter, I can't say I stomach that idea. There has got to be a better way."

"Socialism sure doesn't work," Dana countered.

"I think it's a matter of deep satisfaction from using our God-given gifts."

Dana thought for a while. "I sense a gift in myself sometimes. There are different parts to it, like being at the right place at the right time, or knowing I'm doing or saying what God wants instead of what I plan."

Allen reflected, "There are people who seem aimless, but are closer to the Divine Nature than many persons who we deem respectable society. We don't even recognize their gifts. They walk on different paths."

"Paths in the Kingdom of Heaven."

They pulled into a stone and dirt parking lot. The rustic log restaurant was known for its succulent lake perch. The screened-in porch overlooked the lake. They were happy to see an empty table there.

Allen said, "Just you, me, and the sea."

"With fried lake perch, who could ask for more?" Dana smiled while sinking into her chair.

Dana liked the shelter's early shift. She was a morning person. Also, she was never much help to the cook at dinner or lunch time. She felt more comfortable when preparing cereal and toast.

In the dining hall entrance, Hayden gestured excitedly to Marshall, who was already eating. He went through the line, and as Allen dished him some eggs, he said, "I made a buddy last night at the Coffee Cafe. He have some musician friends. They're gonna back up Marshall."

Allen handed his spoon to Glen, who was distributing hash browns. Dana watched him follow Hayden and slip aside of Marshall. Hayden told Marshall the news.

"I'll call the radio station," Allen said. "I know they want to start as soon as possible. You guys can rehearse at Valley Church. They have an altar area big enough to be a stage, and a good sound system. In fact, we can have a concert there. I've got a good friend who I know will be a big help."

"Thanks, Rev.," Marshall said quietly.

Allen left the room. By the time Dana saw him again, she was in the kitchen wondering if breakfast, with gooey eggs sticking on pots and dishes, was such a good shift after all.

Allen looked chagrined. "I talked with Sandy. The station will record Marshall's CD and advertise. They still get a lot of calls for him."

"What made you decide to help Marshall?"

"Remember Saturday night when you talked about doing what God wants? If I had known ahead of time about Hayden's offer, my answer might have been different."

Dana nodded in understanding.

Then Allen added, "I asked Sandy who puts up the money for something like this. She said they never tried it before from the station itself, but with the interest in the shelter and Marshall, they got an offer from an individual to provide backing."

"Nice. Anyone we know?"

"You might say that. His name is Perry Polk."

WYWH advertised, and Elder Foster helped with the arrangements. They wasted no time, and two concerts were set, one for Thanksgiving night, one for the next evening.

Allen picked up Dana for the show.

"This is a great date," Dana complimented.

Allen smiled. "Thanks, I agree. I bet Gerard didn't take you to anything as good as this."

Dana hit his arm. "No talking about our competition tonight. I think the shelter is the love I'm up against."

"No way. When the board decides on it's new director, I'm out. Back to my lovable druggies. But I'll be dropping by a lot. I've gotten to really like and even admire these guys."

"They are up against a lot."

They pulled into the church parking lot and were pleased to see it full. "I've never been to any Christian rock concerts, but this looks good to me."

Dana was amazed by the transformed appearance of the church. The room was darkened, but colored lights flowed in various patterns. The crowd was mixed with people of all ages and ethnic backgrounds. The concert had been advertised as a fund-raiser for the shelter. It was wonderful to see such support.

The pastor of the church gave a short invocation. He introduced the DJ, Sandy McNeil.

She gave a plug for the shelter then said, "Folks, you know what's coming, because you're the ones asking for him. Remember, I'm the one who discovered him."

Marshall Curry and Band came in. Dana held her breath. They hadn't had much time to practice. The lights lowered more, then spotlights flooded the performers. Elder Foster asked three acquaintances of his to act as security. They sat by the side of the stage, and a few times walked through the aisles.

Marshall now held an electric guitar, as did two others, a man and a woman. Another woman was on drums. They started. The sound was rock, contemporary but not hard. The background vocalists rounded out Marshall's clear, full voice.

"He has what it takes," Allen whispered to Dana.

Dana agreed. "His voice is so solid you can almost touch it."

At the end of the song the people cheered with enthusiasm. Each new song was better than the last, all of them original.

They held a short intermission. Allen noticed some of the shelter residents, who were allowed in for free. Beth had brought them, and was sitting with Sheri.

The lights lowered again. The next song started.

A good angel came one day
  to an unsuspecting town,
He found a man to tell
  that things were coming down.
The man said, "Why'd you tell me?"
  I'm no one they'd believe.
The angel gave his answer,
  "It's time, time to retrieve."

A bad angel thought it fun
  to pillage and to thieve.
He found a man to use --
  his wickedness to weave.
But later on they are gonna learn,
  It's time, time to retrieve.

The amps were set particularly loud. Allen had to shout now. "I wonder what it means."

Dana yelled back, "This is what he was talking about in your office. If he's not lying..."

By this time everyone was on their feet. Many were dancing and swaying at their seats. Marshall somehow exuded energy while staying composed. The crowd screamed for more.

They played two subdued songs for their encore. The crowd quieted a bit, but cheered jubilantly when they finished.

Marshall asked Allen to come up and say a few words for Jesus. Allen was pleased to oblige.

He jumped onto the stage. "To those of you who know God, I hope He put the joy of this music into your heart tonight like He did mine. For those of you who have not yet met Jesus, I pray He come to you and show you His power and love."

"If you feel your life isn't right, you can pray to God yourself. You might not know what you're doing, but Jesus does. One amazing thing about God is that He can teach us as we go along. Jesus is knocking at the door of your heart right now. All you have to do is let Him in."

As Allen descended the stairs, the DJ ran up to dismiss the audience. He spotted Sheri, who was wiping her heavily made-up eyes.

The audience came out into the lobby, in which coffee and cookies were available.

Elder Foster ran up to them. He talked doubly fast. "Man that was something! Best time I had in years. That man, he'll be a great hit, there's no question about that!"

"We're going backstage." Allen directed Dana to the hallway behind the altar. They passed the drummer, whose face glowed with delight.

The room provided for the men to change was open. As they walked in, the other guitar player left. Hayden was inside.

"Congratulations, Marshall," Dana greeted. "You and your group were wonderful."

Marshall closed the door. "You both made this night possible and I'll never forget it. But I know you think I'm lying about who I am. You could have called police, but you didn't."

The singer's sweated face was as serene as ever. "If you like, I will leave now. I'll go to another state and let this whole music thing go."

"What?" shouted Hayden. "Are you gonna let them think you are guilty?"

The veteran turned to Allen and Dana. "This here's a good man and he will never get no more chances like this."

He turned back to Marshall but choked on emotion.

Allen cut in. "Take it easy, Hayden. I think Marshall is thinking of the shelter as well as himself. If he gets arrested, whether he's guilty or not, it will damage our bid to stay where we are. People don't trust the dwellers, and a scandal would play right into the mayor's hands. It wouldn't be so bad if he just disappeared."

"And what about Marshall? I tell you he ain't no criminal."

"Hold on, hold on, I didn't say we would let him do it," Allen answered.

"Marshall," Dana's voice was breaking. "You practically saved my life. Angels or no, I'm tired of distrusting you. We back you all the way."

"We're sorry we put you on the defensive," Allen continued. "Your offer was a courageous one. Please stay and keep singing, friend."

As Allen and Dana drove from the parking lot, Dana confessed, "It's easier to tell someone you'll trust them than to actually do it."

"Lord knows," replied Allen.

When visiting the mayor, Gerard liked to climb the single stairway of City Hall for a short exercise. As he approached the second floor, he saw a small group of persons enter the elevator. He recognized some of the city's top business leaders. He headed directly for her office.

The unlit room was as dismal as the cold, cloudy Friday morning. "What did they want?" he asked.

"They are getting all emotional about the shelter. Some bleeding heart radio station is pushing for it to stay where it is. They want me to back off, but they don't know me very well."

"You better be careful. Are they talking recall?"

"The word was mentioned. They don't scare me. I've been through worse political fights than this, you know."

Gerard knew. "Most politicians with whom I am personally acquainted have skin thick enough to sleep sheetless in the streets. Not that they do, of course."

"That shelter is the key to the rest of the vision, and we will have it."

"I'd be careful about visions, Ms. Mayor."

"If that's your legal advice, good day."

"I have some work to do down the hall. I'll talk with you when you're in a better frame of mind."

Later that morning, Gerard called Dana. He asked her if she'd like to join him for lunch at the Coffee Cafe. She accepted and met him there.

Dana told Gerard about Marshall and the concert. He seemed pleased it went well.

"So how are you doing?" Dana asked him.

"OK, I guess. The mayor sure was having a bad day, though. You'll be glad to know some critical people are backing your shelter."

"That's wonderful."

"I have to admit I was first in favor of converting the building. But after getting to know the people there, I must reevaluate."

"I'm glad to hear that, Gerard."

They sipped their coffee. Gerard looked around, then spoke with a lowered voice.

"I was coming back to the mayor's office to have her sign something. She was on the phone, describing her meeting with the business leaders to the other party. Her voice was agitated, so I didn't walk in. Then Mayor Taylor said, 'You know I don't like to see anyone get hurt, but if you have to do it, get it over with.'"

Dana didn't trust herself to comment. This was a direct accusation. Was Gerard throwing a red herring at her? Granted, Dana didn't like the politician much, but could Mayor Yvonne Taylor actually be involved in something like murder?

After waiting for a response, Gerard said, "I'm sorry. I can see I've upset you. I don't know what to do about the situation myself."

"Gerard, there is some reason to believe that Marshall Curry is Louis Peters."

Gerard looked stunned. "Why on earth would he be living at a homeless shelter? For one thing, the guy is now wealthy."

"I don't know, and I hope it isn't true. In fact, this sounds funny, but I'm telling you this because there are also indications he is not Peters."

The lawyer looked perplexed, then angry. "You think I somehow know Peters hurt Corin and am trying to kill him?"

"No one is immune from suspicion."

They were done with their lunch. He took the check.

"I thought I meant more to you than a suspect on your list."

"Gerard, please."

He walked alone to the register, paid and left before she rose from the table. Had she stooped to using people?

her guilty conscience asked.

Friday afternoon the band prepared for the second performance. Allen and Dana came to watch. Elder Foster called to the couple and led them into his office. He looked shaken.

"That woman on the coast told me where the records for Louis Peters might be. His mother came here from another state after her separation. I just got an answer from a courthouse clerk to some questions I left by electronic mail."

"What did you find out?"

"Louis was given up for adoption when he was eight years old. He was taken in by the Peters family and given their name."

Dana pondered. "Is that a problem?"

"His original name was Louis George Curry."

Dana's throat constricted to choke her reaction.

Allen reeled.

"I know you're shocked, but I've had time to think about this. When Marshall's done, we'll ask him to come to the station for questioning. The guys on security can make sure he cooperates. That way nobody sees the police."

Allen interrupted Foster's plans. "Sandy McNeil called. There will be a national promotion agent in the crowd tonight. If he likes Marshall, he'll want to sign him up immediately."

"Lord, help us," Elder Foster prayed.

As the three sat in disarray, they heard Marshall practice alone.

Will you trust me just a mustard seed?

Our Savior asks tonight.
Will you give up your misgivings?
For you'll see He is the light.

"We told Marshall we'd back him," Dana remembered sheepishly.

"What about Corin Conrad?" Allen asked.

"There is no guarantee she's still safe," Foster stated.

Allen braced himself. "Let's wait for the Lord."

At the Kingsford Condominiums, a lone figure straggled to a door and knocked. Gerard Conrad answered.

"Corin! Corin! Are you all right? What on earth?" Gerard was elated and horrified at his daughter's wonderful, awful appearance.

The girl spoke through sobs. "Dad, I'm sorry. It was the worst. We were in a cabin in the woods and then Louis just left. I was alone for six weeks. I didn't have a car and the food ran out. I didn't know where I was. I walked and walked and finally came to a small town. Thank God I had money for a bus."

The happy father hugged his daughter and guided her into the living room.

"He had a gun, Dad. I was so scared he'd come back and see me leaving." She cried hard. "I'll never run away again."

"It's OK, shh," Gerard consoled. "Why don't you take a nice hot shower, and I'll get some soup."

She blew her nose.

"Corin, I know you must be exhausted, but I must ask you to do something. I may know where Louis is. Can you come to a concert tonight to identify him? He can be arrested for abducting a minor, and possibly a weapons charge."

Corin looked frightened. "I can't. What if he gets back at me?"

"We won't let him do that. You're the only one who can put him behind bars. Think about it as you wash up."

Sounds once again blasted from the Valley Church. Marshall brought forth that voice which pealed like an awakening bell. The standing room crowd shifted gears to dancing room. Dana was lifted to the rafters by the sight of so many people excited for the Lord.

At break, Allen and Dana made their way to Sandy McNeil. She introduced them to the agent/promoter. He was a stocky, cherub-faced man with red cheeks.

"He's just terrif," cooed the agent. "Everything you said. He'll be big before you eat your turkey leftovers."

"Terrif," said Dana, not so sure.

Sandy added, "We'll be backstage right after the show."

"So will we," Allen tried to smile convincingly. "Wouldn't miss it."

As they returned to their seats, Allen had a double surprise when he noticed Beth and Sheri. He didn't expect to see Beth again, and knew she must have paid for her own and Sheri's way. But more jolting was the appearance of the teenager. He wouldn't have known her if Beth hadn't been seated there. Her blouse and jeans were simple and modest, and she wore little makeup.

"We trust in You, Jesus," Allen whispered as the second act started.

Though it was dark, Corin Conrad drank in the scenery from the condominium's windows as she ate two cans of soup and a liverwurst sandwich. Gerard filled another glass of milk.

She said to him, "Is it too late to catch the concert?"

The church-full of fans cheered joyously. The encore did little to settle them. They wanted autographs, and pushed toward the stage. The security men closed in on Marshall. He stayed out on the altar, shaking hands and signing bulletins. Hayden, Sandy and the music agent came to the back hall and waited near the dressing room door, as did Allen, Dana, and Elder Foster.

After about 15 minutes, Marshall asked the other band members to continue with the autographs. He and the guards moved backstage and into the hall, closing a large door to keep fans from spilling through.

Dana headed the group as they approached the dressing room. She felt an emanation from the front of the door and stopped. It was a power so strong it turned her around to face the rest of them. "Don't go in there. It's dangerous," she heard herself say.

Hayden said, "It's OK," as he walked toward the door.

"No!" Marshall warned. He looked above the door frame.

Elder Foster nodded toward the guards. "How about two of you check it out."

One security man stood near Marshall as the other two entered the room. Dana stared tensely at Marshall. A crash sounded from the room.

When the dressing room door opened, a heavily

bearded man emerged, flanked and restrained by two of the guards. A guard said to Elder Foster, "He was in the closet, sir."

Gerard and Corin had gotten through the rest of the crowd to open the backstage door to the hall. The young woman cried, "Louis!"

Dana shot her glance toward Marshall, who in turn looked at the scruffy man.

The bearded man blurted, "Corin!" then clamped his jaw.

The bystanders worked to comprehend. Gerard yelled, "That man held my daughter against her will. His name is Louis Peters."

Dana objected. "He may be Peters now, but his last name *was* Curry."

Marshall stared in dismay at the bearded man. "Louis Curry is my brother. I never knew his adopted name."

Elder Foster, with a look of understanding, said, "Nice work, men. Let's take Louis Peters down to headquarters."

Grief for Marshall filled Dana's heart. She looked at the music agent, who didn't comprehend the matter. Marshall was turning to follow the group. She firmly placed a hand on his arm. "There's someone important here to see you, Marshall. It shouldn't take long. Elder Foster and Mr. Conrad will keep Louis busy for a while. When you're done, you can see him there."

"Let's talk," the agent said to Marshall.

Singer and signer disappeared into the dressing room with Sandy and Hayden. Dana nodded toward Gerard. "I'm so happy Corin's back. Thanks for bringing her here."

Gerard smiled wryly. "I'm sorry I was angry. I hope I can make it up to you."

"My guilt tells me we're even," laughed Dana.

Gerard took Corin by the arm. "Let's go to the station."

Allen and Dana walked to the front of the church, now empty of fans. They poured some coffee and sipped it in Foster's office.

Dana pieced the facts. "The mayor and Louis Peters became convinced they needed the shelter to get their big break. Gerard said the mayor thought a large foreign company would move into Lake City if the shelter were gone. That would've made her an economic heroine. Peters must've realized that Marshall would rally the city on the side of the shelter. He figured he had to get rid of him."

Allen replied, "But the attempts on Marshall started before he ever sang a note on the radio. How did Peters know?"

They considered.

"Say a supernatural being appears to you," reasoned Allen. "He can't perfectly know the future--only God can. But he has more access to inside information than mortals, and perhaps some distorted form of precognition. Once a few of his stock and real estate predictions come true, it must be pretty easy to believe everything he says."

Dana was indignant. "An angel of the Lord would never use that kind of proof. And he certainly wouldn't encourage injury to others for personal gain."

"No, but one of Satan's would. And he got just what he was looking for--ruined lives. A lot of people believe in the supernatural, but have no understanding of the way it works. One of the verses in Marshall's song was, 'It's time, time to retrieve.' 'Retrieve' has several meanings.

In this case, to take what's wrong and make it right."

Dana shivered. "Do you think Peters knew about Marshall being his brother?"

Allen shook his head. He had no answer for that. "One more question, though. Why was Hayden so adamant about Marshall not going to the hospital?"

"I've wondered that myself. I think he and Marshall were both afraid that under pain-killer Marshall might mutter about angels, and be put away."

Elder Foster came back with a wide smile. "Louis Peters already squealed about the mayor. They've picked her up for questioning about her knowledge and complicity in attempted murder."

Allen murmured,

Jesus, you rose from the dead
You are God almighty.
Jesus, it was you who said
the low confound the mighty.

EPILOGUE

Several months into his tour, Marshall came back to Valley Church. When it became clear that the sanctuary wouldn't hold everyone, they all moved to the gym in the new community center the church had just completed next door. Most people kicked off their shoes and never stopped moving.

Finally, at the end of the show, Marshall moved to the mike and said, "I want you to meet one of the people who made it possible for me to serve the Lord with my gift. His name is Perry Polk."

The big man strode to the stage.   "Thank you, Marshall. I just want to tell the folks here that I was a man in trouble. I did some wrong things, and even spent some time behind bars."

"Then, the Lord Jesus said, 'Come to me.'"

The crowd cheered enthusiastically.

"I was so low, I had to crawl, but when I lay at His feet, He changed my life. Any of you who don't yet know Jesus, He can do it for you."

The show ended and Dana, Allen and Elder Foster found their way to the room where they previously arranged to meet with Marshall. Eventually, Marshall entered with Perry Polk.

After some small talk, Dana admitted, "Mr. Polk, you were one of our suspects in searching for Marshall's attacker."

"Perhaps you ahr referrin' to my problem with the IRS. Because I had a record, they kep' a close eye on me. After jail, I got together with a few good Christian folk. I trust each of you to keep a confidence. We founded an active, but secret, group."

"I eventually found how to satisfy the feds without givin' away the whole identity.   I guess the Lord accumulates wealth in some persons for His own purposes. I'm now using my money to support this group in doing God's will."

Dana's brows lifted. Then Marshall stepped over, hugged Dana and Allen. "We're so happy for you," Dana said.

"Thank you all. Pray for Louis. Maybe he'll come around."

Marshall and Elder Foster both pled exhaustion and soon left.

Dana resumed conversation with Mr. Polk. "Last summer I was unemployed and then worked for a short time for a secret group. Their name was 'Faith, Inspiration, Service & Hope.'"

"FISH for short," said Perry. "Perhaps someday God will again lead you to us."

PART III

FISH

FISH MANUAL

Compiled by
Faith, Inspiration, Service & Hope
and the
Spiritual Theory Dept.
Lake City Christian College

INTRODUCTION

Christians believe our prayers can affect various outcomes, as when we pray for better health for a relative. God leaves some things open to our prayers.

The Lord holds destined events unchangeable, and they will happen no matter what we do.

Sometimes He lets us take our work into our own hands.

In still other situations, God uses us as vessels. It is a great blessing to be personally involved in His work.

In Northern Italy, Vittorio Antonelli's ulcer spit fire during the late afternoon meeting. He couldn't show his weakness by taking the prescribed medicine. The board chairman, CEO of Auto Volante car makers and numerous subsidiaries, glared at the Milan managers.

"Were it not for the family, we'd shut the doors today...no, yesterday, the CEO said. "In any case, we must, as the Americans say, downsize."

Vittorio, known as Vic, both resented and pitied the old business leader, who had not shown his face in the last five years. The chairman's final days would see strikes, failing sales, laid off workers.

Finally the meeting ended. The letters offering early retirement would come in the mail.

Vic's pills helped little as he wound his expensive sports car, a product of his company, up the steep hill to his impressive villa. He entered the kitchen and paused there. His wife's minimalist, albeit expensive and faddish, decor contributed to his home's hard-edged atmosphere. Middi, short for Madilina, caught his grimace.

"Ulcer again, or the meeting?" she asked.

"Both."

"I suppose you won't want to go out then, again. We've canceled with the Marcellos twice this month, and tonight they are having a party."

"I can't. You go," he almost pleaded.

"I hate to arrive there alone," she complained. "But, very well. I can't stand another boring night here."

Her petulance had seemed attractive before they were married. It was part of her superb youthful beauty. He desired her long before his wife, related to one of Italy's richest families, died of cancer three years ago. He could barely wait the respectable six months to marry her.

And Middi, a poor, aspiring model and actress, had no better prospects. The 50-ish Vic was still trim and good looking. He was a senior vice president of a car company, with rich and important friends. And his late wife's jewelry looked so exquisite on her own neck, wrists and ears.

Vic was readying for bed when Middi returned. "The Marcellos entertained some interesting people tonight. You know their friend Guseppe, the photographer. He and another man, Harlan Wicklund, are on an assignment for Grandeur, the American magazine. They will take pictures of Italy--homes and prominent people."

Middi almost burst with excitement as she took off her diamond and ruby necklace. She lifted the piece to the light and delightedly gazed at it. "They're coming here! They're going to take a series of me and the house!"

Vic's heart sank. "Middi, who knows how much longer I will work? I don't have money like some of the others. We may move in less than a year."

Unperturbed and still admiring the jewels, Middi asked, "If you're not rich, how did you get these?"

"They were handed down from my first wife's great aunt. Sure, I got my job through my wife, but she was only a second cousin to the business clan. I worked hard and earned my money."

Middi placed the necklace in the case. "They'll be here next Tuesday," she said.

Harlan Wicklund arrived alone at the Antonelli household. Vic tried to stay clear, but Middi insisted he join them.

Harlan set the camera on a tripod. His light blond hair unfurled with it's own will. Turquoise flecks in blue eyes added brilliant intensity. He didn't look much concerned with fashion or finance. "Guseppe's covering Rome and South," Harlan said. "Milan, of course, is the most exciting. The clothes industry to parallel Paris, the financial center to rival Wall Street. They say Milan may be the European Commonwealth capitol."

Vic immediately noticed his sarcasm, but knew it would not connect with Middi. She fluttered, "Oh, yes, Giorgio Armani, Gianni Versace. It's heavenly to visit the shows. And the shops..." Cutting short, she purred, "All the models in this city and you choose me?"

Harlan looked over the patio fence. "Guseppe told me of the beautiful view from your address. He wasn't wrong. If you sit here by the edge, we can get the city with the Alps as background."

Vic felt sorry for Middi, obviously disappointed in his answer.

"What else do you photograph?" Vic asked.

Wicklund looked at him directly. "I'm a free-lancer photo-journalist. For a while I photographed models in my hometown of Chicago, but now I mostly take pictures abroad. I met Guseppe while covering the Italian political corruption trials. Since I had just finished that particular story, he asked me to help with his project."

Middi sat in the chair. Her face reflects her moods, thought Vic. They had married six years ago. She auditioned for every Italian movie and major play since then, getting a few bit parts. Every trip to the city, she noticed more models, teenage girls, gorgeous.

The camera clicked, she changed positions. People would see her, how far she had come. At her urging, Vic reluctantly joined her for a few shots.

Harlan packed his equipment. "Grandeur pays its subjects. You'll get a check and copy of the issue in the mail."

After Wicklund left, Middi drove into Milan.

Jares Ranjah spoke evenly above the revving engine. "We live in two worlds; the obvious physical one and the hidden spiritual. Many people are trying to understand how to live in this second, secret world. They take varied paths, often trying to force the answers. God is blessing our small group. We patiently wait the fruit of His Spirit."

The four-wheel-drive vehicle slid on a dune road iced by Lake Michigan spray. April snow blended into white sand by a winter wind intent on delaying spring. Dana Dushane shifted in her seat. "Why did Perry call us, Ranjah?" She referred to herself and Allen Moran, huddled in the back seat.

Jares Ranjah wore a rough canvass coat reminding Dana of sackcloth. His demeanor seemed meditative, reflective of the India in which he was raised.

"Mr. Polk told the group about you two after he met you. He had strong feeling you would fit well with us. We prayed for several months about it. We waited, and then every person felt a conviction to invite you."

Though it was only early evening, the cloudy winter sky spared no light to a long, wooded driveway of the Monastery of the Mystery. The vehicle retread grooves almost eliminated by new snow. Gusts lifting from the lake's waves found no resistance from leafless trees.

A few monks lived on the monastery grounds. Their only income of one small business enterprise allowed for sparse but adequate living conditions.

For a moment, the dark stone walls seemed to swallow what scant illumination the headlights provided. When her eyes adjusted, Dana saw grounds landscaped with encrusted Chrysanthemum skeletons fenced by shards of ice. Slowly they tread through thick snow and opened the weathered wooden doors against fresh drifts. Leading them into a hall, and down a stone-encased stairs, Ranjah wore even more comfortably his mantle of tranquility.

Faintly at first, ever more clearly, Dana heard a chant of Latin liturgy. Somber yet musical, the few voices blended fully in echo. The jagged currents of Dana's nervousness were assuaged by a smoother stream. After passing this monk's chamber, they came to a candle-lit room. A large man with very dark skin sat at a crude wooden table.

Dana was genuine in her greeting. "Perry! I'm glad to see you again."

Perry spread his hand in invitation. Dana and Allen sat on a short bench. Polk's chair was of simple Shaker design. Ranjah sat on one of the same type by the wall.

Perry leaned back. "Ever since I met both of you, I've felt you might fit into our group. Dana, you're already acquainted with it, since you've worked with us."

"About all I really know is that its name is FISH, which stands for Faith, Inspiration, Service & Hope. The people there were pretty secretive."

"You refer to Eben Stroud and Fuji Yamoto, code names Saber and Flame." Perry got up, then sat on the front of the desk, closer to the couple. He said, "You might call us a Special Forces team. To tell you how FISH evolved, I'd like to fill you in on my own background.

"My folks were very poor, but unlike many Southern Negroes, they didn't migrate to the city. My great-grandfather Amos Polk was forced to this country as a slave before the Civil War. The owner of the plantation where Amos came died in that conflict and left a childless widow. By my father's account she was a good woman, and frightened at being alone. Some of the former slaves stayed on and worked for her. In her old age, she divided the property and gave it to them and their families.

"As I grew, I loved farming the land, but I didn't want to stay poor. The state built rural schools, and even though mine was a few miles, I was happy to walk there to learn.

"I tried my first venture over 20 years ago, but my business soon started to fail. I got low on cash. A few guys I knew ran a car parts scam. You wouldn't believe the money they stole.

"I didn't want to do that myself, but I loaned money and received a few perks from them, like a re-vamped car or two. The whole thing blew, and I got caught in the explosion, for accepting stolen goods. I landed in jail."

Perry's voice was steady and gentle. "Eben was a jail minister from a nearby mainline Protestant church, and conducted Bible studies in the prison. I couldn't believe how those words brought comfort to me then. I came across the verse, John 14:16, 'And I will pray the Father, and he shall give you another Comforter, that he may abide with you for ever.' I thought Jesus must be God to be so close and real."

Dana felt strangely drawn toward this man with so

different a background than hers.

"When I was released, I joined an Evangelical denomination. Eben and I were in separate churches, but we still got together and prayed what was on our minds. After a while, we found we were irritating each other by what we prayed. For example, Eben thought I prayed for my own will and not God's. Also, he told me I was assuming he agreed with me when he didn't. I felt he was afraid to commit himself.

"This problem perplexed us. How could we both be Christians yet disagree on what to pray about?

"But we were both determined to learn and improve. We worked at discussing our differences, praying, and then waiting for God to lead us. We made it a point to try to figure what God wanted, and reviewed the outcomes of our endeavors. It took a lot of patience and the courage to be truthful with one another.

"It also meant using discernment to know when to stand and when to change, which is why we call our technique 'working discernment.'"

"I found I could be honest *and* prosperous in my business. Through God's grace I made wiser decisions. My heart changed, as did my relationships with others. It seemed as though I was learning God's will for me through FISH, and things started to fall into place.

"I knew I needed to give the greater portion back to God. In the meantime, a few more people joined the group from various backgrounds and denominations. We felt God move us into various situations with some wonderful results. We resolved to stay together, and bought a headquarters downtown."

He looked around the small room. "This monastery is a combination of retreat and private getaway. Ranjah seems to feel more at home here than in town."

Jares Ranjah looked on the proceedings with serene features. He lifted his eyebrows and said, "It's also where we conduct our initiation rites."

Perry shifted, and his voice became more forceful. "We prayed about the two of you, and feel God is directing us to ask you to join us." He reached on the table for two loose-leaf books. "Here's a FISH manual for each of you. We'd like you to give us a try."

Dana was excited, but expressed her concern. "I'm not sure I'd really add anything, Perry."

Perry's replied, "God has given us all gifts, Dana. Sometimes it takes a while for them to unfold."

"Though our members are of varying religious groups, each one believes Jesus Christ is the Son of God who came to earth in human form to save us from our sins. Each member believes in the power of prayer. We also believe Christ Himself desires the unity of His followers. If you can be sure of these factors and are willing to make a solid commitment, I think we can provide you with some unique opportunities to serve the Lord."

Perry stood. With his height he looked down on them. "Let's go into the chapel."

Lining the chapel was the same red sandstone used in other areas, but the walls rose twice as high and held delicately expressive stained glass windows. A priest stood on a simple altar and about a dozen monks in the first few pews knelt over small benches. The priest chanted in Latin, with the brothers answering in the same language. Toward the back, several other persons were bent over kneelers. Perry led the couple to a place in back.

Dana wasn't sure how long they were there. The priest gave no sermon. She let the music lead her prayer, felt it stirring virgin depths of her soul. Eventually the brothers stood and filed out. The rest followed, and went to a long narrow dining hall with large wooden cross-beams.

The atmosphere was less formal here. Eben Stroud greeted them as they entered. "Welcome. We are glad to see you both here."

Eben's dark brown eyes were softened by kindness, and his brownish gray beard hid the features of his mouth. His slight accent was American East Coast. He was not as tall as Perry, but heavier.

Several other persons entered, hailed Dana and Allen, and eventually seated themselves.

They served themselves to a simple snack from a modest buffet. Dana wondered if her growing inner satisfaction was produced by the bran muffins and tea or the monastic atmosphere.

As the dishes were carried out by one of the brothers, the members shifted from convivial to business-like.

"If you are willing to work with us for a trial period, we'll start right now," Perry said.

Allen nodded.

Dana said, "Thank you for the opportunity. Oh, what about Allen's code name?"

"Well, we're kind of between Alpha and Armor. Which do you like, Allen?"

"How about Angel?" Dana giggled.

"I think I'll take Alpha," Allen decided, "Even though the first shall be last."

"When do you use the code names, Perry?" Dana asked.

"We don't always use the codes--just in certain circumstances, deciding at the time. My name is Pilgrim.

"There are times when Christians want to stand up and be counted, but times when we want to work behind the scenes. You know, when a journalist investigates other people's lives in the name of 'Truth,' it is accepted by society. But let a Christian become interested in someone, and you can get lots of resistance.

"Also, at this time, several countries are arresting, harassing, and even torturing and killing people who claim Christianity. Sometimes we do work in these types of countries. If our phones are tapped, for instance, we feel the code names would be harder to trace.

"Any other questions?" Perry asked. When none came, he turned to the rest of the group. "At a recent church conference I attended, I met a Ms. Gulker, a member of World Refugee Watch. Perhaps you've heard of the agency--they've got a few books out. She just returned from Dong Rak refugee camp in Thailand.

"The young girls there are being lured to a life of prostitution. Though the central government has grown more sensitive to this problem, some key officials look the other way. The agency made many attempts to stop these agents, but they have not been able to obtain cooperation in this case.

"The camp staff has made some effort to post signs of warning, but these are usually soon removed. Also, many peasants are unable to read. Obviously, the staff has little time and resources to devote to continuing education of each wave of refugees.

"And so we should discern if it be God's will that our next mission involves traveling to the Dong Rak refugee camp."

Fuji Yamoto looked concerned. "Thai is not one of my languages," she said. "We've never ventured into something without at least one of us speaking the native tongue. It could be more dangerous that way."

Eben added, "Also, I've been following a case here in Lake City. It's not a good time for me to drop it."

"Besides," Kathryn added, "we've got plenty of problems in our own back yard. Do we really have to go to Thailand?"

Perry said, "I'm not sure we should split the group since we work so well together. When we sent Ranjah alone to Geneva, we almost courted disaster.

However, for some time before I was approached by Ms. Gulker, the plight of the peoples in Southeast Asia became more visible to me. I read that many of the Cambodian roads, factories, and utilities are destroyed from their civil war. There is massive unemployment, and many women are anemic from malnutrition. All over Southeast Asia, young girls are being lured to the cities for prostitution or the equivalent of slave labor. I feel the Lord was bringing their plight to my attention for a reason.

"The religion of the majority of the population in Southeast Asia is Theraveda Buddhism. As I understand it, Buddha taught that each individual must find his or her own way to their ultimate goal, 'Nirvana'. In essence, they do not believe in God, but more in a oneness with the universe. Though we respect other religions, we believe Christianity holds the ultimate understanding.

"With all those people are going through, it saddens me they do not know our Lord well enough to personally call on Him for help, even though He may silently strengthen them. To help any of them find Jesus' Way would be a welcome task."

Dana watched each person intently as he or she spoke. Though the members were disagreeing, they were calm, almost methodical in discussing their views.

Perry now put up his hand. "Any more discussion?"

No one spoke, so he said, "Let us stop at this point and give it to God." They bowed their heads. "Lord, we want to do Your Will and not our own. We ask you for direction, and trust You to give it to us."

Lori Ren watched her mother, Kear, dexterously weave the stiff palm strips. Kear had grown up in a 'crafts village' in Cambodia, where farming was insufficient for existence. Now she was teaching her daughter to make durable baskets from sparse material. Kear Ren earned their meager living by exchanging the course containers with peasant farmers, who used them to haul their produce.

Lori had always been an attentive student before the death of her father, Tay Ren. He had fallen in pain a few months ago, and no doctor was available to help. Her mother seemed able to work out her sorrow through the baskets' even weaves. But lately Lori found escape by letting her mind wander. Ragtag memories of her family's flight from their first home emerged. It had happened in one of the campaigns during the endless Cambodian Civil War.

As they had fled, the great palaces of Angkor, ruins of a majestic Cambodian empire, rose from the flowered jungle. Angkor Wat sat on the north bank of Tonle Sap, a river lake which flowed southeast in the dry season, northwest in monsoon. Walking past, Lori had felt the unblinking stares of the great stone faces carved by mason ancestors.

Lori blocked the memories of the refugee camps. But she remembered when the battles died down, and the family had walked back on a different road, past small plots of orange trees, rice patties, and sugar cane.

Lori brought her attention back to Kear. Her mother had called to Naat, Lori's brother, to try to find more reeds. Naat did what a 10 year old could do to help.

The sunset ended their work. "We'll take some baskets to the market tomorrow," said Kear Ren.

That night, Lori Ren woke to her brother's screams. Another bad dream, she thought. Not unusual since their father's death.

Then she smelled smoke, and heard other screams outside their hut. Gunfire preceded the whistle of a bomb.

Lori couldn't speak. Though she had experienced an attack before, no preparation could alleviate the terror. From her mattress, the teen-aged girl crawled to her brother. His whimpering stopped when she grabbed his arm. They both moved toward the hut's only other room. Their mother met them at the doorway.

"We must leave again," Kear said. "Quickly, get what we need."

News of guerrilla advances had reached the Cambodian village a few days before. Anticipating evacuation, many peasants piled their meager supplies on ox carts and wagons, to provide at least small comfort in the Thailand-Cambodia border refugee camps. Kear had set aside a full pot of uncooked rice and water container to grab for the trip if needed.

The villagers were running west, pulling their carts, too frightened to cry. The black sky's dark curtains veiled their flight.

More gunfire and shouting erupted to the east. Then, a huge explosion immediately to the south. Pieces of red-hot metal flew past. Lori Ren felt a searing pain across her cheek and forehead.

"I'm hit," she shrieked. In her alarm, she shut her eyes tightly, but somehow kept running. Her mother, a few steps behind, screamed.

Naat caught up and guided her by the shoulder.

"Naat, are my eyes OK?" she cried.

He tried to look in her face as they ran. Flowing blood created a liquid mask. "Keep moving now," he yelled over the noise behind them. "Stay with me. I'll guide you."

The Rens' small village, no more than 100 huts, lay only a few miles from the main road. However, because of the damage from endless shelling and the chance it might be blocked, the refugees decided on a muddy cart trail over the northern foothills of the Cardamom Mountains. They slowly found their way as they had a few years before. Illegal trade had kept the road passable. The route ran more directly to the Thailand camp, but even here they suffered fears of planted mines.

After several miles, the din faded. The Rens felt temporarily safe enough to place their cart aside of the path and try to care for Lori's wound. Her mother removed a cloth from the cart. She started to blot Lori's face. The girl cried out, afraid and exhausted.

"It's OK, Lori," her mother tried to reassure.

Lori tested her fear that her eyes had been damaged. She rubbed them tenderly. Much to her relief, they felt fine, and when she opened them she could see.

Kear patted the injury with the cloth until the

bleeding almost stopped. "The cut runs from your right cheek across the bridge of your nose and above your left eye. Let's continue now. They'll have a doctor at the camp again."

Lori leaned against the side of the cart as they slowly trudged on. The trauma and pain of her injury weakened her. After another hour she could go no further.

Kear pulled off the road, got out a mat and light cover. Below the sheet in the darkness, they listened to the anguished sound of evacuation.

Four years before, when Lori had left her home the first time, she was 10 years old. As they drudged, hot and miserable, she had asked many questions. Why did they have to leave? What were those people doing to them?

Kear explained her own understanding. "The government that held power for many years was so corrupt that the people, the Khmer Rouge, fought and took over."

Tay's anger rose. "The Khmer Rouge were no better. Their hatred went berserk, and they killed hundreds of thousands of Cambodians."

Kear said to Lori, "Many do not like the new rulers, either. The people claim the government is more corrupt than ever. So the Khmer Rouge keep fighting."

"And the farmers must move or get killed," Tay complained.

Now, as pain reverberated in her face and heart, Lori wondered other things. Why is life so filled with suffering? Why does she never feel happy, yet believe that somehow she could?

The next morning felt cool to the loosely clad Cambodians. A breezy 70 degrees seems unhealthy to those used to humid 100. Lori's face drained the energy from her. They stopped several times. Naat suggested she get on the cart, but there was no room, and she didn't want to burden him further.

Others from the village overtook them and passed. Among them was Pao Sno and her brother. Pao, with her large, European eyes, at 13 years old was the prettiest girl in the village. When Lori looked at her, Pao gasped, but smiled at Lori compassionately.

After another day of walking, the Rens reached the Dong Rak refugee camp in Thailand, named for the chain of mountains which cradled it. It was already overfull. Several other towns had been attacked.

The Red Cross and a few other non-government organizations served food, handed out plastic sheets to lie upon, and provided a makeshift clinic. Lori Ren waited several hours for the doctors who first treated patients with serious injuries or signs of malaria.

The doctor who finally saw her spoke Khmer, the Cambodian language, with a heavy French accent. He dipped some cotton swabs with alcohol. "This won't hurt too much," he said. "Your cut isn't infected. You're lucky you weren't closer to the explosion, or you'd have a lot more dirt in it.

"But your wound is starting to close already. It's not wise to stitch it, under these conditions. Maybe someday you'll be able to get plastic surgery for your scar."

Lori Ren returned dejected to her mother. She knew she was not pretty like Pao Sno, whom the village boys clustered around. But how would people treat her now? Would they laugh, or avoid her?

Lori thought of the beggars who had lost their limbs in the war. How terrible it must be without them. At least she was not as unlucky as they.

She cried in her mother's arms. The shy young girl

had twice been displaced from her home, recently lost her father, and now was disfigured because of a conflict which had started before she was born. Though she hardly could imagine it, she longed for a secure life. She pictured herself at home alongside her mother, weaving their baskets, selling and trading them, with Naat tilling chaste fields. If only it could be so.

Vic Antonelli threw the magazine to the coffee table. Middi had been very pleased with Harlan Wicklund's article and left to buy more issues for family and friends. Vic got into his own car and motored East along the A1 highway. Dampness and mist framed the farms of Po Valley, bread basket of Italy. His eyes wandered to farm buildings raised centuries ago. Like me, thought Vic.

He turned toward Ravenna, his home town. Already as a young child, he had been discontent in this agricultural center. He loved automobiles and wanted to work in the factory in Milan.

To earn money as a boy, he worked for the largest cheese and wine producer in the county, Reggi Morini. The eldest Morini son, Emilio, also liked cars. The boys spent hours fixing, breaking, and re-fixing tractors and other implements on Reggi's huge estate.

Reggi was a lover of land and its yield, a believer in hard work and accumulation, a simple man. But Emilio, belying tousled, farm-fresh features, was attracted to the urbane.

When Reggi died, Emilio had the money to put ideas into action. He built a chain of upscale restaurants. His marketing was slick, and the sales grew. Unlike many Italian businesses, he offered stock to the public for his wine, cheese and restaurant corporation. Emilio became known in Milan's financial circles.

Now Vic pulled his car off the street beside Ravenna's Basilica di San Vitale. The city had long ago been western seat of the Holy Roman Empire. Its buildings dazzled the eye and imagination with millions of pieces of gold-embedded glass formed into mosaic representations of Bible stories.

Vic again thought of the old days. He had made his way to Milan, worked long hours at the car factory and took management classes. He met and married Gina, rose quickly in the family-run plant. He and Gina were unable to have children.

In the early days, Emilio and Vic met with young men occasionally at one of Ravenna's pubs. In his drunker moments, Emilio shared secrets with the group.

"Never forget the politicians," he pretended to whisper. "They serve the people just like our waiter here and they like tips."

One year, Vic and Emilio had entered a trans-Europe antique car race with a restored auto from Auto Volante. Emilio, thrilled upon winning, swore he'd put his best friend in his will: leave him his antique car collection. Vic laughed. Emilio had always been busy with his business. He owned a run-down 1960 American Chevrolet. Besides, Emilio was a only a year his senior.

The friends parted ways. A few years after the race, they bumped into each other in Milan once and had a drink in a dark pub. Emilio told Vic he'd finally had time to put into restoring a couple of antique cars. His younger brothers had sued for more control of the company.

In his old whisper, but with sadder countenance, he said, "Remember, Vic, love is everything."

Vic walked slowly, then submerged into the Galla Placidia Mausoleum.   The vault's starburst blue sky projected into mosaic saints who held their arms to him, robes flowing beneath.

Italy's determination to clean up corruption had caught up with the Great Morini. A brokerage associate of his was already jailed. Accused of political bribes, Emilio had committed suicide in his posh villa three days before his trial.

Vic sat in the mausoleum without thought of time, then returned to his car. He drove along neighborhood streets, then past fields of his youth.

He tried to imagine successful businessmen who had never passed money. He wondered how far down the corporate ladder the investigations would go, and which rung he stood upon.

The mail over the next few weeks changed Vic's life. First was notice of mandatory retirement.

Vic was crushed. The business partners had ignored not only his years of faithful work. It was like a divorce, a total rejection of the part of the family he had been, still felt himself to be.

When he cleared his office, his pain no longer confined itself to his stomach. He ached for his youth, not as much because it was gone but for the blindness of it. But still he couldn't grasp what went wrong, why he had never known it would come to this.

A few days later, two large envelopes were delivered. One was addressed to Vic, one to Middi.

As always, Vic retreated to his den to read his mail. He was curious about the large envelope. It was from a prestigious Milan law firm.

Dear Mr. Antonelli:

Because the family of Emilio Morini has inherited all but these two items from his estate, and considering the circumstances by which he died, the will has been found acceptable to them and will not be contested.

Vic's stomach churned. He didn't want anything from Emilio. He would only be reminded, feel the intense guilt. As many good times as they had, he could only ask himself why he hadn't been a better friend. His breath caught at the glance of the next page, with a picture of an antique car. He knew it immediately, but read the description.

Type 57G Bugatti racing car, winner of 1936 French Grand Prix. From Bugatti collection.
Estimated value: $1,300,000.00.

His heart racing, Vic turned the next page.

Duesenberg Convertible Phaeton, 1934. Burgundy with leather interior. Originally owned by Victor Emmanuel III, king of Italy.
Estimated value: $2,500,000.00.

Vic hadn't time to collect his thoughts when Middi burst into his den screaming, "Who the h--- would send me these? What do I have to do with any of it? Get those d--- things out of my sight." She threw several large glossy photos with the envelope onto the floor. She stared at him few seconds before running out the door. Her pale, sick face scared him.

Vic looked at one of the pictures which faced up. It showed a teenage girl completely emaciated and with large, purple patches of skin. She stood in front of a plain white building with several palms leaning in various directions.

Another showed two young girls, also emaciated, lying on woven grass mats. They looked dead, and a few persons stood by, crying. They all had Asian features.

The fallen envelope lay front up before him. No return address, sent from Pattaya, Thailand.

Vic slowly picked the pictures up. The others showed scenes of a resort town which pricked long-unused segments of his memory.

Vic's skin crawled as he wondered who could have sent these pictures, and why. He had temporarily forgotten about the cars.

Dana and Allen emerged from Allen's pick-up in front of a tall, bay-windowed home. First grand, then dilapidated, then restored, the gabled house at which the couple now stared stood a few blocks from Lake City's modest but historical downtown. The door, framed in carvings of the trees from which its substance came revealed through a glass window the oak floors, stairway and balcony within.

The lumbering rush of the late 1800's brought professional wood toolers among the groups of immigrants to America's Lake Michigan. Most homes of their handiwork were now gone, through fire or neglect. A few sections of the city retained the buildings these European craftsmen created.

Perry opened the door. The couple followed their

host to a living room of spacious dimensions. On one end, a wood and tile fireplace contained a moderate fire. A few area rugs complemented wood floors and wainscot.

A delighted Dana smiled at her host. "Your new home is very nice, Perry. Lots of character, like you."

Perry Polk's white teeth sparkled. His southern accent emerged only when he endured a compliment or great stress. "Ah'm very glad to see you both, too. Please make yourselves cahmfortable."

Allen and Dana found a stuffed love seat next to French doors which led to a plant-filled sun room. The other members were already seated.

Perry started with prayer. Then he said, "We will continue the discussion we started at the monastery. But first, let's tell Dana and Allen a little bit about ourselves."

One woman was Kathryn Tanis. She was in her 50's, medium height and build. Her short, stylish hair was a shade greyer in front than in back, and her facial features pleasantly rounded. "I grew up on a farm about 10 miles north of Quebec," she told them. "I studied biology and physics at a University there. I had several American friends who invited me to a discussion group about the Catholic faith after Vatican II, which was a meeting of priests from all over the world. The emphasis had shifted to spirituality at the lay person's level. I felt moved to learn more. Now I have an interest in learning how science and religion mesh. Eventually I found my way to Lake City to teach at LC's."

"Elsie's?" Dana asked.

Kathryn laughed. Haven't you ever heard Lake City Christian College called by its nickname? L C C C, or LC's."

Dana smiled and nodded.

"I live in a house east of the college. I had lived in a trailer for several years, not knowing whether I'd stay at LC's. But when I got a longer contract, I moved to a one story home. It's east of the campus, near the golf course. I play golf about once a week. I'm not very good, but I like the exercise and I'm getting better."

Perry gave the background on Saber, Eben Stroud. He graduated from Wharton in Economics and had been an administrator and business manager in various situations. Eben added, "I already told Dana I enjoy reading theology."

Flame was otherwise known as Fuji Yamoto. Born in Japan, she majored in foreign languages in college. She had a desire to live in the U.S. She worked as a translator for U.S. Immigration, and became a citizen.

"Fuji has an interesting background," Perry added. "She was brought up as a Zen Buddhist, and became involved in New Age in California. Then she heard Jesus calling to her by name. St. Teresa of Avila described this type of experience in her book, *Interior Castle*. She called it a corporeal locution, a type of vision. It took Fuji a while to sort through her experience, but she eventually answered. She is now a member of a local Pentecostal church."

Fuji added, "I live in a winterized cottage on Lake Michigan. It's got its own little beach. I bought it during the economic slump in Lake County, before real estate started rising."

Perry said, "And Ranjah recently returned from Australia's Outback. He goes there to be alone with the Lord for long periods of time."

Dana shook her head. The group was so impressive she was intimidated. "I was born in little old Lake City," she said sheepishly. "I'm not an expert at anything."

Perry laughed gently. "Remember, Dana, that I

came from a very humble beginning. It seems God has a special affection for the little people."

Kathryn then said, "Getting back to the business at hand, I had some thoughts on the problem of whether to go to the refugee camp. Perry, isn't your hobby photography and filming?"

Perry looked intrigued. "It certainly is. I think I get your drift. We could introduce ourselves as a group interested in filming the camp for a documentary. For that matter, we could distribute the film to church groups when we get back."

Eben said, "Since we talked, I've been thinking about the apostle Paul. He didn't stay in one place, but took young Timothy with him far across Europe and Asia."

Fuji looked intrigued. "Still, some people stayed behind, at their 'home churches.'"

Perry nodded. "Kathryn, classes are almost done for this semester, aren't they?"

She nodded. "The Christmas break was short so the college could start a building project early this spring.

To the group he said, "Dana, Ranjah, Kathryn and I could go on this mission. Allen would be a good addition, too. Eben and Fuji could carry on here. I am feeling conviction to try it this way. Do we have agreement all around?"

Dana caught her breath. Could they really be going to Thailand? Everyone nodded.

Perry prayed and praised. "Thank you, Lord, you are among us. How wonderful for us that is!"

At the Dong Rak Refugee camp, the Wans made a sleeping area for themselves in one of the long bamboo shelters. Because Thailand also housed Laotian refugees to the north and Burmese to the west, their supplies were strained. The one meal per day consisted of half-filled rice bowls.

Soldiers fitfully patrolled the area. Orphan babies cried for their loss until exhausted. Lori tried to forget about missed meals by attending to other children.

After a few days, Lori noticed a new young man in camp. He didn't look like a refugee, but emitted an air of confidence and control. He was neatly dressed in Western-style clothes.

She noticed him approach Pao Sno. Her heart sank. Never would a man like that be interested in her. She resumed babysitting duties, and was shocked when the young man and Pao called to her.

"Lori!" Pao said. "This is Fang Rachathon, from Bangkok."

With head bowed, Lori ran to them. She shyly stole glances at Rachathon. Though in his late teens, his face was mature. His hair's unusual swirl pattern lent him an air of sophistication. He seemed to know he was handsome.

Fang talked in a low, confidential tone. "Twenty five years ago, my mother, Uon Rachathon, migrated from Burma to Bangkok. She wanted to supplement her family, as had many other women from this country just west of Thailand.

"My mother became a waitress, and sent her clan as much as she could. It was more than they usually saw in the provinces, and helped them greatly. At first she had planned to go back to Burma, but after I was born, she wanted to stay."

Fang Rachathon's voice changed from smooth to smothered. "My father did not stay with her, but I think she always hoped he would come back. He never did."

He relaxed again. "As I got older, she had saved enough, with my small income as busboy in the same restaurant, to send me to the school at the Buddhist monastery, a practice done by many young Thai men. She had even suggested I could afterwards enter the University. Mother always wanted more for me than the lives of most men in the neighborhood.

"But I had other plans. If Mother wanted me successful, I'd do it my own way. Theraveda Buddhism never did anything for me and I wasn't going to waste my time."

Armed soldiers emerged from a nearby tent. Fang glanced at them nervously and whispered, "Let's meet again tonight after the sun sets."

Lori could hardly wait for the appointed time. The tiny portion of her meal made little difference. When she finally found them, Pao Sno stood by a lantern, her face radiant.

Fang Rachathon stared at Pao, indulging himself on her beauty. He started speaking to her of the Eastern and Oriental Express, one of the world's most expensive and luxurious trains. "Southeast Asia's rolling mansion," he said, "two overnights from Bangkok to Singapore."

He had seen the E & O come in when boarding his train to the camp. "Several older passengers debarked, elegant and bejeweled," he related. "They gave way to two of the most lovely Asian women, dressed in formal evening wear, I had ever seen. One of the passengers approached them, and thanked them for their wonderful service. He gave them some bills, which they happily accepted.

"I could get you a job there," he exclaimed. "You would be married to a rich young man within a year!"

Pao was obviously excited. But her mood broke when she looked at Lori.

Fang Rachathon talked quickly to Lori. "You, too, could make a good living in Bangkok. Many house girls are needed. You will make enough in a few years to do whatever you want."

The girls promised to talk with their parents. He urged them to meet him in the morning. They would have to walk four miles to the train station. "From then your life will change," he bragged.

Lori returned to her mother and told her everything. Her mother started to cry. "What will I do without you, my daughter?"

"I will be back, Mother, I promise. I want to earn enough to buy good supplies for our baskets, maybe even to put a shop in a village. Then we can buy good land for Naat. You know he loves to farm, like Father did."

Lori felt there was something else pulling her, but wasn't sure what it was. She knew she couldn't make everything right by herself. How could she stop the war and destruction by making money? All she wanted was a simple life, yet she felt an urgency to take this opportunity to go to Bangkok.

Her mother seemed to sense her feelings. "You are a good child and never ask for much. I will let you go if it is your desire."

Lori Ren, Pao Sno and Fang Rachathon arrived in Bangkok the next day. Fang hailed a taxi outside the station. He told the girls he had a place for them to stay until he could speak to the right people. He brought them to an area of run-down shanties and took them into one of them.

"I've got everything in here you need," he said

before he left. He locked the door on his way out, which made Lori nervous.

The girls were very tired, though, and had little trouble sleeping after they helped themselves to some dry goods in the cabinet. Fang was back the next morning. "The people at the Eastern Express were real interested in you, Pao, but they don't have an opening right now. We've found a way for you to make some money while you wait. Lori, you stay here a few more hours, then I'll take you to your new job."

After they left, Lori again became anxious. Her stomach churned and she couldn't eat. She could only look out the shacks tiny windows and watch the dirty children play.

Fang eventually returned, and spoke roughly to her. "Time to go. Don't think of giving me trouble, like your friend did."

Lori's heart sank. What had happened to Pao? Where would he be taking her?

They drove out of the back alleys and into the always congested streets. Lori had never seen so much humanity, or imagined the traffic. They started climbing hills which overlooked the huge gulf inlet of the South China Sea. How would she ever find her way back to her mother?

The homes were getting larger, gardens more lush. They eventually turned into a long driveway blocked by a gate and high fence.

Lori Ren's first sight of the house in which she would serve filled her with an eerie foreboding. It's white stone and glass structure looked like a cross between a fortress and hotel. Were there really people endowed with the power to amass so many resources around themselves?

They drove inside the compound, which included the huge main home, several guest houses, large garage and implement barns.

Hundreds of flowers and bushes surrounded the road and buildings. Fang seemed pleased with himself. "I told you I would get you a maid's job with a rich family."

A small houseboy, about 12 years old, ran out to greet them and take her bag. Lori Ren felt the strain of the trip and dreaded meeting her masters. She worried what would happen to her if she couldn't please them.

She stood there a few minutes, afraid to even look up. Finally, she stole a few glances. The home was luxuriously furnished, with many displays of collected articles. There was Chinese porcelain in cases, and sparkling vases of jewel and silver inlay. But Lori's eyes were drawn to a single object on the floor next to an ancient-looking stone statue, and her wonder turned to excitement.

Tanung Onong, the home's mistress, came to the drawing room. She looked at Lori Ren's face. "What an ugly scar," she commented. "No matter, you won't be seen much anyway."

The boy translated in embarrassment.

"There are many servants here," Onong said. "Your work will be reasonable. You will clean, do laundry and help in other ways when needed. Now Mahidol will show you to your quarters."

Lori was relieved when the boy led her out of the main house and to one of the separate dwellings. It looked older, like it may have stood alone for years before the present owners developed the land.

He took her up teakwood stairs to a second floor. The house was modernized inside, and her quarters contained a bathroom which had to be explained by Mahidol. Lori marveled at the amazing luxury. The large window allowed light and air into her roomy living/bedroom.

Her heart leapt at the view. The many flowers and trees framed the open water of the Gulf of Thailand. She grieved for her mother and brother, wishing they could see this, too.

But her mind turned to the object she had seen in the masters' house. A basket of rich, soft reeds with a scene, subtle in hue, of oriental sailboats on a mystical mountain lake.

Dana, Perry, Kathryn and Allen flew in a Polk, Inc. jet to O'Hare airport. Ranjah had business in Chicago, Perry told them, and would meet them there to leave for Bangkok on a commercial line. Dana had flown a few times now: her trip to Geneva and a round trip to Jamaica, her mother's birthplace. She had loved it and didn't mind the long hours in the plane. She still remembered the thrill of sighting several whales in the Atlantic Ocean.

They processed their tickets and baggage. Perry had purchased tickets for non-adjoining seats. "Never know if you might sit with someone who needs a Christian by their side," he said.

They ate a few bites at one of the canteens, then moved into the gate area. Dana saw Ranjah standing among the waiting crowd.

"All passengers boarding Flight 202 to Milan, now loading at Gate G."

As they boarded the jet, Dana wondered if it could fly as high as she.

After two movies and several meals, the plane landed in Milan, Italy, for refueling. A few passengers left, then others boarded. A man in his 50's sat beside Dana. She had rarely seen a face so drawn and gray. She wondered if he was ill.

After they took off, the man read some, lay back a short time, but seemed restless.

Though not shy, Dana had trouble starting conversations with strangers. She thought of Perry's purposeful seating arrangement. Let me be a vessel if I can, Lord. She took a deep breath, then said, "Do you speak English?"

"Yes," he answered. He turned toward her as though glad to talk.

"Ever been to Bangkok? This is a first for me."

"I went there for many business trips, but that was 20 years ago. My company, Auto Volante, was expanding into Asia."

"Oh, yeah? I've always wondered what that name meant in English."

He looked sad even when he laughed. "It means flying car. We wanted the sporty image."

After a pause, Dana said, "You must know people there, in Bangkok."

"Yes, there's a friend of mine, a woman. It's been so long." He faltered for a moment, with a pained look. Recovering, he asked, "What is your purpose there?"

"My company will be filming a documentary on refugee camps. We'll land at Bangkok and take land rovers northeast to the Dong Rak camp."

He offered his hand and said, "My name is Vic Antonelli."

"Dana Dushane. Glad to meet you."

"Have you ever heard of the Oriental Hotel? It was the best in the world in its day. Some say it still is. That's where I stayed on my business trips. I will go there now, retrace my steps I suppose."

A stewardess came with their meal. They didn't speak much more, and after they ate, Dana felt very tired.

"I'm afraid I'm going to have to rest if I want to avoid too much jet lag," she told him.

"You are right, same for me."

The plane landed before Dana was fully awake, but when she saw the taxiing jets from all over the world, she became very excited. Still, she was reluctant to say goodbye to her new friend.

"I hope you find what you are looking for, Vic."

"Thank you, Dana. So do I."

The airport was a mixture of every nationality. It took the group almost an hour to get their bags and pass customs. When they walked out of the building, the sauna-like heat surrounded and pressed upon them.

"Whew," said Perry. "This is worse than Georgia! There's our ride."

The Refugee Relief agency had sent a Land Rover and a transport truck. The drivers were Thai, dressed in military shirt and shorts.

"Welcome," said one of the Thai soldiers. "We will take you Americans to the camp." His English was stiff-mouthed and guttural.

The drivers talked as they loaded the baggage into the back of the military truck. "Our government needs help to support the people who flee here. Other problems in the world have taken attention from our plight. Yet people are driven from their own countries on all our borders; Burma, Laos and Cambodia. We become overloaded."

Perry and Ranjah rode in the rover.

The other FISH members climbed in back of the truck. It didn't take long to realize the truck's shock absorbers were not designed for a smooth ride. They started and stopped in jerks as motorcycle taxis continually cut them off.

The city's stifling and polluted air clutched at Dana's throat. It seemed the humanity would go on forever. In fascination, she watched the life on the khlongs, or canals used for streets, business, and recreation on every kind of boat. The small vessels held colorful produce and products for commerce; there were even floating restaurants where a cook made meals while people waited on boardwalks by the water.

At last the vegetation of the country came to view. The green of the rice fields almost glowed, so fresh and pure. Water buffalo wallowed in lowland mud. Flowers abounded in colorful trim. Everywhere, thatch huts stood on stilts. The dry, cool season was ending. Rain and heat would make the rice grow.

Then the terrain became hilly. Eventually they could see through the canvass that they were approaching the camp. Dana was thirsty and had a headache. Now the acrimonious smell of chemical disinfectant on top of organic waste and decay turned her stomach. It was getting late, and she hoped Perry would let them acclimate before beginning the work.

The drivers brought them to the journalists' barracks, a long thatch skeleton with mat floors. They unloaded the equipment and covered it with tarpaulin. A lone writer tapped a laptop computer at a rickety card table.

Dana breathed relief when Perry told them their work would start the next day.

A photographer entered with cameras slung over chest and back. He observed the new group. He looked so intense as to be intimidating. When he sat down on a cot and removed his cameras, he seemed to relax a bit. Allen introduced himself first to the reporter and then headed toward the photographer.

Allen's baseball playing past still manifested itself in a muscular build. His outgoing approach was so enthusiastic as to appear aggressive to some. "Allen Moran," he said with hand out held.

The man looked almost relieved that Allen didn't hit him. "Harlan Wicklund," he returned.

Each time Lori Ren walked from her room to her master's house, the effort increased. At first, when hopeful her mistress would be kind, she quickly tread the path, looking forward to serving. Now, after a week of translated orders and insults, she fought crushing waves of internal resistance. She suffered nausea and light-headedness, and was almost unable to eat.

Tanung Onong had the houseboy tell Lori she was expected to understand Thai. He helped her as much as he could, but had work of his own. Lori tried to please Tanung, but was criticized whether she waited for orders or worked without them. Tanung wanted her clothes on a hanger one day and laid over her bed the next. Always she told Lori she should know by now how to do it. She said she would tell her husband to call the agent to take her back to become a prostitute, since they didn't have to have any brains.

Lori was scared. Much as she didn't like her present job, she couldn't stand the thought of being with men who forced themselves upon girls. After another distressing day, she climbed into her bed but couldn't sleep.

What am I going to do? wondered Lori. I can't run away. I don't know anyone. Maybe I should just try to get to the sea. I can't swim. It wouldn't take long.

But the thought of never seeing her mother or brother again stopped her. She had to hang on and get back to them somehow.

The next day, Lori was relieved that Tanung announced leaving for a few days with her husband and taking no attendants. They got through the packing, with Tanung screaming that all her clothes would be ruined from wrinkles the way Lori was packing them. Before they left, Tanung told Lori to help one of the other maids with her work. She had bought material for them to prepare decorations for an upcoming party.

The Thai maid, a diminutive middle-aged woman, was in a basement workroom, cutting patterns of fish, fruit, and other shapes out of a silky paper. Then Lori caught her breath. A pile of reeds were laid out in a corner. They looked soft and supple.

The woman got through the idea to Lori that the mistress wanted a basket for a centerpiece. Lori excitedly volunteered to make it, hoping the maid would show her what to do. The maid agreed, and started the bottom coil. Lori had never seen a basket stitched instead of woven. Some reeds had been dyed, and the maid attended Lori periodically to show her how color could be added. Lori was thrilled by an emerging swirl. The basket was starting to resemble the one upstairs, though not, of course, as fine. As she proceeded, Lori's inner peace returned.

Vic entered the small, dark restaurant, sat at a corner table. He was shocked by the decline of the neighborhood. Twenty years ago it was fresh, jaunty, fun-filled. Now vague despair clung to the faded walls.

An older waitress handed him a menu.

"I just want a Scotch. Can you tell me if Jah Patham is still here?"

She hardly glanced back. "I will call her for you."

His heart leapt. He never thought he'd trace her, and now in moments would see her face.

Before his drink came, another woman approached. A grey streak ran through her black hair, which she had arranged in a twist. Her eyes were lowered, but rose in disbelief when he said, "Jah."

He asked her to sit with him.

"I am working," she replied in English, the language they both knew.

"A few minutes, please."

She sat and looked at him directly. He took her hand. "You are still beautiful," he breathed. But he knew he was looking at an embittered person. "Do you hate me, Jah?"

"No, I don't hate you. For many years I loved you."

"I am so sorry, Jah. I don't know why I have lived my life this way, hurting so many people, letting them down.

The drink came. "Please talk with me, Jah. Let's have dinner. Like old times."

"All right. Tonight."

Vic drove his rented BMW off the main streets to the address she had given. He went past khlongs choked with weeds. Dirty children fished the mucky waters. Bangkok's polluted air mixed with sewerage odors.

Jah wore an old-fashioned, Western-style dress. Vic was embarrassed to think of Middi, who wouldn't be caught dead in last season's styles. They drove to the Oriental, then took a boat across the Chao Phraya River to the restaurant.

After ordering, her face darkened. "Vic, I must tell you something. There is no good way to prepare you. I have AIDS. I found out a few months ago. I have not yet told anyone. I am afraid I will lose my job."

"My God," was all he could choke out. He didn't want to insult her by asking if she was sure.

The appetizer was served. How could he eat? he wondered.

"I suppose I am lucky to be living as long as I have," she said. "The girls now--they have so little chance.

"The sex industry here makes huge money, and though the national government says they try to stop it, some local officials do all but promote the operations. There are police who won't arrest the operators or pimps. Some of them use the services themselves.

"The young men see the money to be made as agents. They go to the country, trying to entice young girls. They lie to them about what they will do here. Their families are so poor and desperate, they are easy to convince."

Jah became angry. "The district is not like it was when you were here, Vic. Before, the women made their own choices, earned enough money to go to school or leave. Now children are brought here, 10, 12 years old.

The sex tourists don't want disease, so they ask for virgins, younger and younger girls. The helpless victims are abused, get AIDS, are shipped back to their villages to infect others and die."

Vic's stomach turned. A severe, fiery pain exploded in his gut. He leaned toward the table, as Jah gasped. The restaurant, the world, blackened at the edges, as dark blades lanced his heart.

When Vic regained consciousness, he found himself on the floor, with the waitress and Jah trying to loosen his tie and shirt to give him more air. He felt terribly embarrassed and got up quickly. He reached for his wallet, but the maitre d' by that time had approached and told him he need not pay.

"You should go to a hospital," Jah said.

"No, no, I'm fine.

Jah pulled him onto a boat, and they eventually stumbled back into the Oriental lobby.

Vic said to Jah, "I'll just rest here a few days. I want to see you again."

"Very well. I will talk with you tomorrow."

Perry, Dana and the rest had slept on top of their own sleeping bags set on simple cots. Dana stiffly rose at dawn and tried to remember where she was and what she was doing there. It all slowly came back, and her next job was to relocate the facilities she finally had found the previous evening to wash and change. The director of the camp had told the group to use the military base which stood about half a mile outside the last camp tents. Dana was glad to see a somewhat modern setup, compared, especially, to what she had imagined.

Kathryn was also rising, so they left together. The camp seemed eerily quiet compared to the evening before.

Kathryn said, "Last night I was thinking about what it means to be dislocated from your home and everything familiar. I've been uprooted myself, although not in a situation like this. It's a long story, but it took me a while to find a new job, and my money dwindled to a pretty small amount. Even with my faith it was a tough time."

Dana commiserated. "I don't know how people get through life's hard times without faith in our God."

"It literally must be hell."

By the time Dana and Kathryn returned, Perry and the rest were checking their cam-corders. They set off to do some filming, and Perry tried to relocate the English-speaking director to interview.

The group filmed through the morning. They had decided to meet back in the tent in the early afternoon, hoping they could speak and pray in privacy. They had just started when a wail rose from outside. A woman shrieked inconsolably. They ran to the area where others had already gathered, trying to help the woman.

"What is it?" Allen asked Harlan, who had also run to the scene. "You speak Khmer?"

"Yes, I do. Someone just told her that the man who took her young daughter to Bangkok last week is an agent for prostitutes. He had lied to them. These people are naive, a common problem. She is helpless now, since she wouldn't be able to follow or trace them."

The members of the group watched as the woman sat with legs crossed where she had stood. She put her head in her hands, and did not respond to the others who spoke to her.

Perry gathered the FISH members back into the empty journalists' building. He started praying. "Lord, here we are. We've come a long way. What is it you want us to do?"

They stayed in prayer for a few minutes, thanking God for their safe journey there and praising Him for his goodness to them. Just seeing the turmoil here made them all appreciate their own homes.

"I thought perhaps the Lord would lead us to some government officials whom we could convince to help these young girls," Perry mused.

Allen said, "God thinks differently than we do. Though He sent us all this way, He may use us for just one person."

"Every soul is a great jewel," Kathryn added.

They sat in prayer for a time.

Perry took out his Bible and leafed through it. "I'm thinking of a place in Matthew. I found it, it's chapter 7. Jesus says, people will say to Him that they did great works in His name, and He will say He never knew them. Not everyone who cries to Him shall enter heaven, but those who do the will of His Father."

Dana asked, "What if the mother has to leave the camp for her homeland before her daughter can return? They may never reunite."

"To say nothing of what may happen to the girl's soul," Allen added.

"Are we all agreed that this is the opportunity God wants us to take?" Perry asked.

"I feel it in my heart," said Kathryn.

The others nodded.

Perry prayed, "Lord, it looks like this is it. Please

break the strongholds which might keep us from moving where You want us."

"Let's take our time and see what develops," Perry said to the group.

They sat, prayed and talked for several minutes.

Ranjah said, "I am going to find out the family's names and town in Cambodia they come from. I feel I must go there to intercede for the girl."

"That's very dangerous," Allen warned. "The rebels have kidnapped and killed Britons, Australians and Americans because those countries are supplying arms to the government."

Ranjah smiled benignly. "I have before done intercession prayer in remote and hostile territory."

Kathryn added, "He seems to have the nature to survive nature."

Allen shook his head. "But can he survive vicious terrorists?"

Ranjah left to look for Harlan Wicklund to interpret more of the mother's information for him. The rest decided to disperse and continue the day's filming.

In the evening, the group was winding down, readying for sleep, a few reading by lantern light. Harlan Wicklund returned to the tent. He placed some film rolls into one of his camera cases.

"Do you have a special interest in refugees?" Perry asked Harlan.

Harlan sat on his cot. "Not so much that as the Cambodian people. I've spent a lot of time with them. They are a wonderful, happy people, but they have another side. When the people in power take out their anger, it's the peasants who suffer. I photograph them and send pictures to papers and magazines of richer nations to try to get them interested in helping.

"Society has to change.   It's bad enough that international businessmen have to have their perks and take as much as they can.   At least they are somewhat productive. What really gets me is the spoiled rich women who do nothing with their lives but redecorate their homes and go to fashion shows. What about people in the world who have no money for simple sanitation and medical facilities?"

Dana listened closely. Her impulse was to argue with him. After all, she thought, many wealthy socialites raise millions of dollars for charities of all kinds.

But she thought of the FISH manual: *You don't know the situation like God does. Ask the Holy Spirit what to say or do.*

Holy Spirit, please show me, Dana prayed. Then she heard herself ask, "What brought you to Southeast Asia, Harlan?"

"The first time, I had an assignment with a major news weekly in Cambodia. That was about 10 years ago. I always wanted to do foreign assignments. I guess it seemed adventurous and exotic. But I really got to like it here, like I belonged here. I myself have become Buddhist, like most of the Cambodians. We need to become at one, and remember that this life is illusion.

"I worked for a while in other places, but I always wanted to come back to Southeast Asia. After three years I decided to go freelance and, for the most part, stay. I only left for a short time to go to Italy, to cover the corruption trials."

Allen spoke up. "Harlan, do you know the name of the agent who took the girls with him?"

"All I know is, he tells the girls his mother made

lots of money as a Bangkok waitress." He got a pen and paper from the camera case. "Here's the name and number of the friend I'm staying with in Bangkok. I've been developing my film there. If I can be of further help, let me know."

Perry and the group finished filming. They asked the refugee camp director if he knew the name of the agent who took the girls away. The director said he knew some of the agents, but he did not recognize the description of this one.

The group returned to Bangkok the same way they came, and asked the driver to take them to the airport. Their bags were put onto a luggage dolly, which they rolled into the building.

"Ranjah is flying to Phnom-Penh," Perry told the rest. "From there he will travel Northwest to the town from which the Ren's fled." Ranjah extracted a small backpack from the dolly.

Dana asked Perry, "Is it necessary to go to a geographic place to pray? Can't God hear us anywhere?

"That is true, and for most of us, the place that matters is within our hearts. But for some, location prayer is like a pilgrimage. Often, Ranjah feels special clarity when he humbly follows a call to a locale."

They bid Ranjah goodbye. Then, reemerging from the airport, the group hailed a taxi.

In the early planning stages of the operation, Eben had contacted the Christian Relief agency located in Bangkok. This was a worldwide agency with which FISH had previous dealings. He arranged for accommodations in case they were needed.

The group arrived at the Christian Relief building complex. The front entrance connected with the main hospital. Perry asked for a Mr. Evart. After a few minutes, they were led to his office.

"My friends!" Mr. Evart exclaimed. "It is so nice to meet you in the flesh." He was not Asian, but looked like he might have come from India or Pakistan.

After introductions, the administrator said he had arranged for two rooms in their staff house. "I'm sure you will be comfortable. Our whole staff is committed to our Christian mission. On the way, let me show you our facilities."

They followed him through the corridors, and Dana noticed how young the patients were. The nurses wore rubber gloves and masks in the patients' enclosed rooms.

"Our primary function is to nurse AIDS patients. None of the other hospitals want them, they had nowhere to go.

"Like in the states, many HIV-positive persons are drug addicts. Many of the women here were prostitutes who started so young that their tissue is easily damaged. The virus penetrates and infects them. Often they become pregnant, and their babies are infected."

Dana looked in dismay at the young faces. What chance had they been given to know what life could offer? She was thankful that in this clinic they would be told of Jesus.

They went to their rooms. Mr. Evart gave Perry a room he used when he stayed at the hospital for emergencies. Allen shared his with an orderly.

Dana and Kathryn had their own double. The room contained two small beds, each with bed stand and bureau.

Kathryn exclaimed as she folded her clothes into the

drawers, "I don't care if we only stay one night. I hate living out of a suitcase, or in this case, a backpack!"

Dana laughed. "It will be great to sleep on a regular bed. I never thought I'd be so thrilled to be able to use a washing machine. I'm even grateful for the sterile hospital smell."

Kathryn sat on her cot, stretched and breathed deeply. "I'm in my 'meditate and pray' mode."

"I'll walk around the grounds," Dana said, "but can I ask you something first?"

"Sure."

"How do you think it is that you, FISH members, come to agreement? And what happens when the group doesn't agree on what to do?"

Kathryn responded, "God is too complicated for us to understand, and we are all unique. Yet I know how it feels in my own life when I ask Him what to do and try to wait for Him in my decisions. I continue on with that in our group.

"The difficult part of seeking Truth is that with each step we may each have to face the internal pain of change, to fit into God's mold. I believe that accepting the pain of being totally honest with myself is a critical part of my physical and spiritual process.

"I've been working for several years at the theoretical level on the feedback systems the Lord may have created within us. I believe Truth has an energy of its own. It affects my breathing and muscular movements. If God guides our paths on earth even in part by physical means, it follows that we may be able to sense that guidance. For example, human beings make emotional attachments and actually feel them in our bodies in various ways, as though something is happening physically.

"Getting back to FISH, each individual has diverse experiences and knowledge. A group can discuss the pro's and con's of a problem to give more of a perspective, and each person contributes his or her own ideas of what is happening.

"If the FISH members don't come to an answer during our meeting, we wait for a while to see if our minds and feelings undergo the internal changes I just mentioned. God often brings all persons to His plan, so that the whole group would have the same thoughts and ideas. This takes patience and time on our part.

"But agreement does not always happen. Sometimes we just honestly don't see eye to eye on a solution. We wait, and in some cases don't do anything.

"Then there is another possibility. We 'agree' to submit to each other, which Paul advised in the Bible. Submission is very difficult; if done for the right reason, and is far from wimpy. It can take great internal strength to submit, and may even be the test for whether an individual can belong to a group like ours. Some people always want their own way, or always believe their way is right. But if we don't give in sometimes, we get stuck in our own worlds and are unable to find God's Truth and Way.

"We at FISH humbly realize we are deeply dependent on God and each other. There is a feel for when to submit and should be done more often than we want to recognize, and this means men as well as women. Again, the decision depends on the individual being able to understand God's communication, because one does not really agree with what is being done, but allows it anyway. There is a peace for the submission deeper than our opinion.

"The feedback system I was talking about is

important for knowing if we are on the right track. It takes experience to distinguish between feelings of personal power and those gifts of the Spirit which Paul tells us about: gentleness, kindness, love, humility. Physically, I feel the difference between peace, when my muscles stretch and relax, and stress, when they tense and cramp. But there are not direct correlations even there. If discernment were easy, we'd have it all figured out by now. I think God speaks to believers individually, and there may be many different systems, just like there are different kinds of computers."

Dana nodded, realizing it would take a while to think these ideas through.

Kathryn resumed, "Another dynamic applies to a feedback loop for trust. The members of FISH accept that God is the only one who completely understands each situation. We realize how easily humans, even Christians, can be deceived. It's important to allow the Lord to move and guide us a step at a time. Though we are blind, we can walk with Him to the goal. Therefore, complete trust in God is really the bottom line. And that is open to anyone, no matter how smart or how lowly.

Many Christians acknowledge contradictions in the Bible. In working my own theories, at times of frustration I become peaceful by remembering that God's ways are described as 'unsearchable.' One of the most beautiful aspects of the lives God designed for us is the sense of mystery. Humans are naturally curious and will always be trying to learn more, but no matter how scientific we might get, *love* supersedes our understanding.

"It is an utterly amazing God who can protect and guide so many of us, His children, as we go about our lives. And yet I believe He can and does."

Dana sat for a few moments, then rose to leave. "I believe so, too."

Mr. Evart had told the FISH group that visitors were allowed in an outdoor garden which served as a courtyard lounge. Dana walked there now, enjoying the palm foliage. She was delighted to find orchids growing along a flat stone walk. Some simple benches surrounded a fish pond. A pavilion covered a few benches near one of the hospital buildings.

Several teenage girls talked with each other in Thai. One was very emaciated, another supervised a baby. Still, they looked in many ways like typical teenagers, curious about the world around them and desirous of happiness in their lives. Dana sat there for a while, wondering how the devil could be so mean.

When she returned to her room, Kathryn was up.

"As upsetting as it is to imagine the problems of these people, I have to admit I'm hungry," Dana rumbled.

Allen was at the door. "Thai food!" he said when they opened to let him in. "Gilbert and I are starved."

Kathryn laughed. "I'm not ready to eat yet. How about bringing something back for me? I'd like to see what I can learn here. I want to find someone to interpret."

"I told the orderly I stay with, Vuth, about our mission," Allen said. "He happens to have been born in Cambodia, and speaks three languages."

"Wow, you've been doing homework already!" Kathryn exclaimed.

Allen and Dana walked the crowded streets. After all this time, she finally had him to herself.

Though they weren't in the best section of town,

they didn't want to go far to find a restaurant. They came upon one with a dingy look but good smells.

"At least this should be cheap," Allen chirped.

Dana's hunger overcame her distaste, so they sat down at a small table and looked at the menu. Dana found the Thai language unfathomable, the letters looking like ant mounds with the little ants crawling below and other insects flying above. Fortunately, many Thai shops catered to English and Chinese speakers also. The menu was printed in sets of three languages.

They ordered Mee Grob, crispy herbed noodles, and stir-fried curried pork. Dana admitted the kitchen's fragrances tantalized.

She started to feel tired from the eventful day. "You know, Allen, I was kind of surprised you decided to give FISH a try."

"Hey, anyone with a fish hanging around their neck should be a member of a group called FISH."

Dana's eyes adjusted to the semi-darkness. "I guess after getting to know Perry, the way he helped Marshall Curry when we worked at the homeless shelter, I couldn't help but be intrigued. Then when I found he was involved in the same group I had worked with before, I started to feel like God was telling me something."

They were silent for a while. Dana enjoyed Allen's company.

Several tables held other diners, and to Dana's back, a few men sat at a bar. She overheard snatches of conversation. To her surprise, one voice seemed familiar, accented in Italian.

"Allen!" she whispered. "There's a man at the bar. You won't believe this, but I think he sat with me on the plane. What a coincidence!"

Allen tried to observe without staring. "Million to one coincidences are more likely God's designs."

The man got up and moved toward the door.

"I'll be right back," Dana said as she jumped up. Outside the restaurant door she called, "Vic!"

The man stopped and turned.

"Remember me?"

He looked guarded, then smiled a bit. "Of course, from the plane."

"Would you mind if we talked again, maybe breakfast tomorrow?"

"I have some things to do tomorrow, but, yes, that would be fine. Meet me in the Oriental lobby at nine."

By the time Allen and Dana left the restaurant, a rich moon illuminated edges of silken clouds. Allen put his arm around Dana, and she felt a deep warmth which had nothing to do with the ambient heat.

"Full moon over Bangkok," he said.

"I can't believe we are here."

On a bridge by a khlong, they stood and watched late boats move homeward.

"Isn't God awesomely creative?" Dana breathed.

"I'm sure glad he created you." Allen tilted his head toward her. They kissed above the Chao Phraya River's surging sway.

The next day, Dana took a taxi from the hospital and entered the Oriental lobby, an oasis on another already sweltering day. Vic walked toward her. He directed Dana to his rented BMW, and drove to an elegant restaurant.

Dana was glad she had packed a simple skirt for the trip. Vuth loaned his vintage iron, and she had pressed it on the bed. Black and hemmed just above the knee, it complemented her healthy, natural appearance. As usual, she wore her hair tied back.

After ordering, Dana spoke in low tones to Vic. "I'm so glad you agreed to lunch. I hope this is not too personal, but I wondered if you're well. On the plane, and even now, you look quite pale."

His tired face managed a smile. "Thanks for your concern. My ulcer gets more vicious, but I didn't know it showed."

He sipped on some milk. "To be truthful, Dana, my life is, how you say? in shingles."

"In shambles?"

"Yes, that is it. I always thought I do good if I work hard, make money to get what I want."

"Life is not so simple, is it?" Dana asked gently.

"No, I am finding out. My wife now--I get what I deserve. She loves money, not me. The people who really loved me I took for granted, even ignored. And now it is too late."

He stopped and placed his hand first to his lower chest, then to his forehead.

"I'm sorry if our talk is upsetting you, Vic." Dana half-rose to attend him, but he raised his other hand to stop her.

"I'm OK, just a small spasm."

The waitress delivered the rest of the food. They remained silent a few moments as they slowly ate.

"I found my friend," Vic said. "She is waitressing, as she did when I first came to Thailand. I'm afraid she is ill."

Dana laid her fork on the plate. "How difficult this all is for you. Have you been able to find a church among all the Buddhist temples?"

"I'm afraid I have not gone to church in a long time. Not since my mother took me in Ravenna as a boy. And then her funeral."

"Would you go with me? There's a chapel in the complex we're staying. I think they conduct a service every morning."

For the first time since Dana met him, hope showed on Vic's face. "Yes, I would like that."

As they drove to the hospital complex, the buildings changed from modern to older wooden fronts. Several women dressed in skimpy outfits stood on one of the porches over a canal.

"Another thing bothers me," Vic said. "My wife got some pictures of people in hospitals somewhere in Thailand or Southeast Asia from an anonymous sender. She has no involvement in any way I can think."

They arrived in the chapel a half hour before the scheduled service. During that time, they knelt and prayed. Dana heard Vic's whispers, "I am so sorry, my God. I am so sorry."

After Vic left, Dana sped to find the rest. They weren't in their rooms, so she went through the halls. She finally saw them emerging from Mr. Evart's office.

"Let's go to the courtyard," Allen suggested.

Dana shared her experience with Vic. Then Kathryn said to Dana, "Ranjah called. He told us to find Harlan Wicklund and talk to him."

"About what?"

"He was cryptic, as usual. He told us he visited Angkor Wat, the great ruins. He said, 'The roots of the jungle trees strangle the Buddhist Temples.'"

The four sat in silence. Then Dana said to Allen, I think you should go. Harlan seems hostile to women.

"Let's both go. I'll do the talking."

Kathryn said, "That agent who lied to Lori Ren and Pao Sno is our only chance to find them. Mr. Evart told us which patients in this hospital are Cambodian. Perry and I hope to talk to them through Vuth. Perhaps we'll find a connection."

Allen called Harlan and the photographer agreed to see them. The couple took a taxi to the other end of the city where utilitarian cement buildings provided lower middle class apartments. At their first ring, there was no answer. Allen buzzed again, and after another moment, Harlan answered, somewhat frayed. "Sorry to keep you waiting. My hands were immersed in developer. Have a seat."

Tables and chairs were stacked with pictures and magazines. A few rope lines pulled across the living room were hung with pictures of art, buildings and landscapes.

"Just push the photos to the side," Harlan said hastily. They're not organized."

An understatement, Dana thought. She declined his offer of juice, as did Allen. As she pushed and lifted the pictures, she caught a glimpse of an unclothed girl with a disturbing expression on her face, lying on a cover-less bed. Behind her was a middle-aged, overweight man.

She handed the photo to Allen. His stunned face turned from it to Harlan as the photographer turned with his own drink.

Harlan looked at the picture in Allen's hand and said with a high laugh, "Some of my friend's more covert work."

Dana felt Allen crackle with fury. She braced herself for an outburst. Instead, Allen put the picture on the table and sat down, visibly fighting to regain control. She and Harlan sat also.

"Harlan," Allen started, "I don't believe you are aware that we came to the Dong Rak camp in behalf of a Christian organization."

"Oh." A slight blush in Harlan's light coloring belied his indifferent demeanor. "As I told you, I am Buddhist myself. I am becoming one with all things."

"Well, to be truthful, buddy," Allen's voice was level, not sarcastic, "I have no desire to be at one with the likes of this."

Harlan blushed more. "Those girls earn a lot of money, and send much of it back to their poor villages. They like foreign men. Some of them even get married."

Dana wanted to yell out in anger, but Allen's demeanor inspired her to be cautious. "Harlan, look at this girl's face."

Harlan glanced at the picture a few times in silence.

Allen spoke. "I know you have pity for the Cambodians. We want to find the girls that were taken from the camp. You won't change the situation in Cambodia by allowing innocents to be forced into lives they didn't choose."

The photographer's brows knit and lifted as he listened to Allen's words. He sighed and said, "The agent is Fang Rachathon. I heard his name from a soldier in camp. I don't know where he lives or anything else, I swear."

Allen stood and Dana followed. She had a small New Testament in her pocket. She smiled at Harlan and said as she pulled it out and gave it to him, "Be at one with the Three in One."

He took it and Allen added, "Thanks, Buddy."

As they walked into the streets, Dana looked at Allen in admiration. "I guess I've always been suspicious that you were the self-righteous type. I think I've been underestimating you."

"You and the FISH Manual are good influences."

The FISH group returned to the central courtyard of the Christian Relief complex. Perry and Kathryn had made little headway. None of the girls in the hospital recognized the agent's description. Allen wiped sweat from his face as he described the encounter with Wicklund.

They seemed to be at a dead end. Dana sat on the edge of her bench and bent over, watching the fish in the greenish water. She felt like a failure. Perry had spent his time and money bringing her and Allen all the way to Thailand, and what had they produced?

For some reason, a section of the FISH manual came to her mind. "If you get a cut on your hand, you give it attention. You wash it, put salve on it, bandage it. When you feel pain in your heart, give it attention. Let God wash it with Living Waters."

Dana took advantage of the group's silence to focus on the ache in her chest. She felt herself relax and breathe more deeply. Her neck rotated very slightly back and forth. She tried not to think at all but trust, trust in God.

A picture of a phone came to her mind. A phone, *my phone...*

Dana tryed not to get too excited so she wouldn't over-interpret her thoughts. Also, she knew that God didn't always provide answers this fast or in this way.

She prayed silently, *Heavenly Father, if this picture*

*is from You, please bless it and help us to follow through,
that You may be glorified. If it is a deception, please open
my eyes to it.*

"I might have something," Dana said.

"What is it?" Kathryn asked.

"Do you know, I bought a phone with an answering
machine a few months ago, and it was made in Thailand!"

Allen and Kathryn exchanged dubious looks.

"My phone has a remote operation code. If I call
my own number from another phone and put in the three
number code, I can have the messages play to me. I have
the instruction card that came with the phone in my wallet
right now."

Allen was becoming interested. "That could work,
but a three number code gives us 1000 possibilities for
Rachathon's phone."

"True," Dana said. "It is a long shot. But if he has
the same brand of phone as I do, maybe we have a chance.
The factory builds in its own code, which stays the same
unless you take the time to change it. If he's like me, he
didn't bother."

Allen nodded. "However, there's still a small
problem. He probably doesn't have a listed phone number."

After a pause, Kathryn said, "The agent's mother is
a waitress. She's been working in Bangkok for over 20
years. Dana, didn't you say Vic's friend is a waitress? By
some chance they may know each other."

"Another long shot," Perry said. "Bangkok is home
to over 5 million people, you know."

"That's half a million waitresses," Allen quipped.

Dana sighed. "Still, back home waitresses move
from one place to the next. I've done it myself. After all
these years, Jah may have crossed paths with Rachathon's

mother. If the number isn't listed, let's call Vic and see if he will arrange a meeting with Jah."

They did call and Vic complied. He phoned back and told them to come to his suite that evening.

Jah had already come to the suite when the group arrived. She looked wan, sitting on the stuffed couch. Vic had ordered pitchers of iced tea and coffee and invited them to sit. In the midst of opulence, Dana's concern for the missing girl crackled like kindling.

Vic sat by Jah and said, "Explain to both of us."

Perry took over, telling them the situation starting from the refugee camp. Jah covered her face, clearly moved.

Perry finished. "We thought you may know of this young agent, or perhaps his mother. We would like to know where he lives, or if you can get his phone number."

Jah sat still a few moments. She finally stirred. "I remember the boy's name. I know his mother. She worked at Bangkok Wok a few years ago. The last I heard, she moved to a place on Patpong Road, showing girls to men through a large window."

"Jah," Allen spoke gently, "Mr. Antonelli told us of your illness. If you could help us find this girl, you may save her from the same fate."

Jah nodded slowly. "I will try."

The group left.

Vic poured wine for himself. Jah declined a glass.

She took a deep breath. "Vic, a few months ago, a tourist happened to leave a magazine at the restaurant. I saw you and your home in it. After all these years, I still had your address." Jah put her head in her hands. "I sent your wife an envelope, with pictures."

Vic reeled. He looked at Jah for a long moment.

"You sent those photos?"

"I took them at the clinic I go to for my illness."

She shouted, "I was angry with you, with your wife when I saw that magazine! I am dying and alone. You live happily on in comfort."

Vic spoke in a soft voice. "If it's any consolation, Jah, I do not live happily." He turned from her, looking out the window to the ever-bustling city.

Jah sat back. "Why did you come to Bangkok, Vic?"

He tried to think logically, but knew his decision had not been based on reason. "I guess, when I saw those pictures of Asians..."

"You saw their misery and thought of me?"

Much as he wanted to avoid her question, her accusing eyes, he knew he could run no longer. Shame enveloped him, but his gut no longer pained. He faced her and said, "Yes, that is true."

His unexpected honesty pierced her long-held defenses. She cried openly.

He ran to her, afraid of her rejection but determined to show his care. He touched her hand lightly, and his emotions brought his own tears. "I have lived so many years without senses, without true care of people. I don't know how that happened. I only learned of it recently, when my own misery came."

She looked at him, tears streaming. "Your own misery?"

He nodded and felt safe enough to enclose the tiny body with his arm. He told her of his sour marriage, the termination of his job and death of his friend.

"And now your illness, Jah, is more difficult than all the others. It was stupid of me to think things for us could be the same as before, but I still feel deeply for you."

Then, suddenly, he brightened. "It may be hard to believe, my little one, but your despair can be turned into hope.

"Just today, I attended chapel at the Christian Relief hospital. That brought me back to my youth, when my mother would cover her head with white lace and take me into Ravenna's Basilica.

Vic's eyes glistened with the vestige of his tears. "How I had loved my family and friends then, with my youth's whole heart. All this time I've been trying to better myself when already God had given me what I needed.

"Come with me tomorrow to the church at the hospital, Jah. I will tell you of my religion, which is so different from the one here. I believe in a God who loves all people, and gives eternal life to those who understand and believe what He did for us."

She listened intently. She said, "In Buddhism, we do not think a God exists. We must work at our own salvation, and if we don't reach Nirvana, we must come back in another life to try again. But I am scared. I don't want to come back to another life which may be even worse than the one I've had. Yes, I will come tomorrow."

Vic felt hope and peace surging within him. He and Jah held each other into the falling night.

At midnight, Vic drove Jah down Patpong Road, an area well-known for it's fleshly wares. Jah looked back and forth then exclaimed, "That's it, that's the one where Fang Rachathon's mother works, or at least did work, the last I heard.

They stopped and went in. Men lined a bar upon

which a young girl, barely covered, danced. Vic asked to see Mrs. Rachathon. He and Jah were led up a narrow stairs to a hotel-like hall. The waiter knocked on the door. A woman in her fifties opened the door. She had a worn, dirty bathrobe falling over her thin shoulders.

Jah spoke to her in Thai. Mrs. Rachathon shouted something, then lowered her voice and talked, agitated, for several minutes. Jah rebutted her argument in a pleading tone.

Mrs. Rachathon spit out several short words and closed the door. Jah said to Vic, "She wouldn't tell me where he lives. But I have his phone number."

The party given by Mr. and Mrs. Onong could be considered a success by the number of compliments they received. One of the guests especially praised the centerpieces of baskets filled with freshly cut flowers.

After a sumptuous dinner, the party-ers started to disperse through the patio door to the compound's grounds. The guest impressed by the baskets approached Mrs. Onong privately. "I'm having a dinner party myself next month, and I'd like to have your girl make centerpieces for me."

Mrs. Onong was aghast at the thought of introducing Lori to one of the high society of Bangkok. That she, Tanung Onong, would have a scarred, uncivilized servant who couldn't even speak Thai seemed incongruous with the rest of her perfect household. Tanung replied, "You would be welcome if the girl is still here. She's homesick and wants to leave Bangkok."

After all the guests departed, Tanung told her husband to call the agent to come for the girl. She was loud and plain enough so that Lori, who was cleaning up in the kitchen, heard. "Let her be a prostitute," Mrs. Onong said. "They won't see her scar in the dark."

Mr. Onong, only wanting peace in his household, complied. He told her he'd call first thing in the morning. She insisted he do it that moment.

They argued for a short time about the hour, but in the end it was done her way. He was surprised Fang Rachathon didn't answer. Mr. Onong left a message on the answering machine, reminding the agent of his address.

When it was very late, after the Onongs had retired, Lori finished up alone in the kitchen. She wanted to run away, but didn't know where to go, and at the moment was too tired to try. Perhaps she would be able to escape later. She might need money, though. Or, she rationalized, something she could trade.

Lori came into the living room and stood still, listening to make sure no one stirred. Then she tiptoed to the basket that laid almost hidden by an ancient floor statue, picked it up and took it to her room.

The next morning the FISH members were joined in church service by Jah and Vic. Dana felt the grace of the Lord who had gathered them from all corners to come together in united love. She was silently joyous for Jah, sensing the new life which was starting within the woman.

After the service, Jah gave them the phone number. Vic invited them to his suite at the Oriental. They accepted and asked Jah if she would translate the messages for them if they could get through. She agreed.

Dana got out the instruction card for the answering machine she had at home. She had never even tried getting a remote message from her own phone, since she waited to come home to get her messages. She dialed the number and prayed the agent wouldn't answer. It rang a few times, then she got a recording. When the recording was done, she pushed the three numbers for the factory code. Then she pushed the 1 button, the number function for playing back recorded messages.

Dana could hear the tape rewinding! She quickly gestured to Jah, who took the receiver from her hand. Jah had a pencil and paper, and wrote down the messages.

When Jah hung up, Dana couldn't contain herself. She wrapped her fingers into a raised fist and shouted, "Yes! It worked!"

Perry was also pleased. "Looks like a lot of messages, as if the agent hasn't been home for a while. Perhaps he's on another trip for new girls."

"Or maybe he doesn't erase his messages very often," Allen said.

Kathryn couldn't wait. "What do they say, Jah?"

Jah started with the first. "I need two young ones, Fang. You know where you can reach me."

"Supply and demand," Allen said contemptuously.

"This one says, 'The last one was sick when you brought her here. We want healthy ones.'"

"I'm not sure I want to hear these," Dana said, getting sick herself.

Jah agreed. "I think this may be one we can do something with. It's a man who says his wife is not satisfied with their female's housework. He wants the agent to pick her up, and left an address."

They looked at one another. Perry said, "She might not be the one we originally were looking for."

Allen said, "This is the agent that was at Dong Rak camp. He might take this very girl into prostitution instead of another housekeeping job."

Perry nodded. "If we can do anything for her, let's try."

Vic gave the keys of his rented car to Perry, who would take Jah and Dana to the address. Jah would tell the girl's 'employers' they were friends of Fang Rachathon. Perry told the rest to go back to the hospital and bring Vuth to the hospital courtyard.

"If the Onongs don't buy our story," said Perry, "at least they're not likely to call the police. But they may threaten. We'll have to leave fast if things go badly."

Dana shuddered. She had heard stories of Spartan Bangkok jails.

They found the address. Perry whistled at the massive home and grounds. He parked in front, and then put up his hand to stop them from exiting the car.

"We had better ask the Lord to cover us.

"Lord, surround us with the light of Christ and seal us with the cross of Christ. We claim His victory over death and darkness."

They emerged from the car and approached the door.

The boy answered. "Is your mistress at home?" Jah asked.

He brought them inside and called for Mrs. Onong.

She came, looking displeased.

Jah spoke to her in Thai. Mrs. Onong nodded and called to the boy.

Tanung Onong asked them to wait, not offering a seat. It was only a few minutes when Mahidol came back with a very slight female. Her face was directed downward so far that one could see only her forehead and the beginning of a scar above one eyebrow. She held a small, bulging bag.

Mrs. Onong gave instructions to the boy and left with a curt nod toward the group. The boy spoke to Jah, who then took the girl's arm and headed toward the door. Mahidol opened the front door and they trouped out of the house. The houseboy opened the car door for Jah and Dana took the frightened teenager in her arm and placed her into the back seat with her. Perry started the car and drove away.

While the others breathed sighs of relief, the young girl started crying. Jah turned to her and said some things in Thai. Then Vic's friend turned to Perry and said, "I told her she will be OK, but I doubt if she can understand much Thai."

Dana gave the girl a hanky and held onto her hand, trying to console with her touch.

Once at the hospital, they led the girl to the garden and she sat on a bench beneath an open roof. They brought her some water, which she drank shakily. Vuth talked to her in Khmer, and she calmed a bit. She shyly answered his questions.

Vuth translated to the rest. To their delight, she was indeed Lori Ren from the Dong Rak refugee camp.

"Praise God," Perry said excitedly. "I do believe we found His will."

Vuth continued. "She said her mistress told her she would now be taken into prostitution. I informed her that the people here were able to outsmart the agent, and they want to help her get back to her family."

Lori started to speak excitedly and started crying again.

"There's one problem," Vuth said. "It seems she stole something from the house."

Perry told Vuth, "Will you ask her to show us?"

Lori gingerly pulled the basket from her bag. She repeated a phrase over and over.

Vuth translated, "She says she is very sorry."

Dana realized that being jailed in any country, especially as an exile, must be a horrible experience. She'd hate to see Lori kept from her family for a foolish action done in panic.

Vic looked at the basket. "I'm familiar with some antiques. I'm sure this is 18th century or older, from Japan. It is probably quite valuable."

As they conferred, Lori hung her head. She knew inside her heart it was wrong to take other people's possessions. But others were always doing that to her.

Still, she felt very bad. Here were people who she didn't know that were trying for some reason to help her. Why had she hurt her own chances?

Lori asked Vuth to explain to her who these people were. He told her, "They try to do God's will. They do good things in the name of Jesus."

Jesus? Lori wondered.

Allen took the basket. He said, "Let me take it to the police. They don't have to know who actually stole it."

"You'll be called an accessory," Dana warned.

"We'll just see what happens," he said, going for the door.

"I'll come with you," Dana yelled.

Allen and Dana entered the police building and asked the first person they saw for an English speaking officer. Apparently they were understood well enough, because they were led to a small room where the policeman behind the desk asked, "May I help you?"

Allen gave him the basket, saying it was not his and he wished it be returned to the owner.

The policeman asked them to wait, took the basket and left. Dana's palms sweated along with the rest of her as 10, 20, 30 minutes went by. A question continually ran through her head: How are you going to explain to your parents you're in a Bangkok prison?

The officer finally returned and said forcefully, "This is a stolen object."

Dana's heart sank, but Allen spoke up. "I guess you could say that, but it isn't stolen if we return it, is it?"

The policeman, in no nonsense fashion, said, "It was stolen from the storage warehouse of the Tokyo Museum of Art in 1987."

"In Tokyo?" Dana redundantly asked.

"Where did you get this item?"

"I can write the address for you," Dana said, pointing at his pencil and pad. "A house girl picked it up from there and gave it to us."

The policeman perused the address and then the couple's faces. "I will need your names and addresses, as well as the house girl. I assure you we will check on your story with the utmost of care, and I don't want any of you to leave Bangkok."

Dana was never so glad to emerge from a building. They went back to the hospital, and were happy to see that the group, including Vic and Jah, had waited for them in the garden. Lori had been given a room to recover from her scare. Another pleasant surprise was that Ranjah had returned and sat with the others.

Dana and Allen joined the group and told them of the events at the police station.

Vic said, "Lori told Vuth she just wants to go home, make baskets and have a simple life."

He sighed and shifted on the bench. He asked them, "Have you ever heard of a Duesenberg? It was the epitome of car design from America, that land of wonders.

"I loved cars, new and old. I loved the way they worked, and the power they had to move us. To me they represent man's ingenuity. I was so attracted to cars that I let myself live with and for them. And for the things I thought that should go with them, like beautiful women and an expensive home."

"I own a Duesenberg now, and I haven't even looked at it. I will sell it and my other holdings. And though, how you say, the battle is up the hill, I will try to start a business of importing baskets from Southeast Asia to Italy. They will be beautiful quality, with the best materials the world can offer. Perhaps we will get into other goods, too."

Kathryn smiled at Vic. "And I bet you'll help your employees to find a good life."

"The best life," Vic smiled and looked at Jah, "in Jesus. We will try to help other girls and boys like Lori. Come on Jah, I will take you home."

Jah and Vic bid the rest goodbye. Vic asked Perry to arrange with Lori to notify the hospital of her permanent location.

As Vic's car stopped in front of Jah's home, he said, "Little one, I am sorry. My heart is with you. But because my wife and I made a union before God, I feel I must do what I can to save my marriage.

Jah looked down. "I think I understand."

"And yet, now my business will bring me here often, and I intend to visit and help you."

She smiled and put her small hand in his. They sat in the car for a very long time.

Perry made arrangements for Lori Ren to be escorted back to the Dong Rak camp, despite his fear that the police would press charges over the stolen basket. While he was still in Mr. Evart's office, a police officer entered and asked for Dana, Allen, and the house girl. They were summoned while Perry waited anxiously.

Upon their arrival, along with Kathryn, Ranjah and Vuth, who all crowded into the office, the officer said in English, "We uncovered a Bangkok-based international art theft ring at the address you wrote down. Hundreds of stolen articles were found in the home and grounds.

"The laws in Thailand concerning antique export are very strict. Many artifacts are being stolen from Cambodia, brought across the border and illegally sold all over the world. We had suspected many of these items were here in the city, along with other stolen artifacts. This is why we had a matching picture of the basket. But we didn't know who or where the ringleader was.

"We do not think the agent Fang Rachathon was involved, but we are looking for him for questioning about his own activities."

The officer turned toward Allen. "Because you recovered the basket, you are entitled to a 90,000 yen reward."

Perry threw back his head and laughed. Allen, looking chagrined, accepted the check.

Dana said, "Let's see... that's about $1000.00. Once that is exchanged into Cambodian currency, I'll bet that will go a long way in relocating Lori's family."

When the officer left, Perry explained to Lori, through Vuth, that she should keep the hospital informed of her Cambodian location so Vic could contact her about a new basket business.

Lori didn't understand. They were going to try to help her first back to her mother, then in a basket-making business?

An unfamiliar feeling of well-being started to fill Lori Ren. Aside from their unbelievable willingness to help a stranger, there was something different about these people. They were peaceful, confident in a quiet way. She cried again, this time for joy. Lori looked at all the others, then asked Vuth, "Who is Jesus?"

The group, FISH, prayed in the hospital garden at the end of a very long day.

"Thank you, Lord," Perry started, "that tomorrow we fly home."

"Amen," Kathryn said. "We thank you, Father, for your wonderful plan and exciting guidance. We pray for the souls of Vic Antonelli and Jah Patham, Harlan Wicklund and Fang Rachathon. We pray for Lori Ren and her family, for peace for them in Cambodia."

Allen added, "Also, dear Lord, we pray for the young girls of Thailand. Will you give them strength to endure, and allow them to hear and know you."

Dana was thrilled to feel the cooler air of Lake City upon disembarking the final flight of the journey. Never again would she complain of West Michigan weather, at least not until next winter.

On the plane, Perry had set the date for the next meeting. He asked Dana and Allen to think about working for FISH full time.

Allen drove Dana home from the airport. "What do you think?" he asked.

"I think I'm very, very tired."

"No, about FISH."

"It's pretty unconventional, but I like it."

"I feel the same way."

When Dana got out of the pick-up, she could feel the magnetism of the comforts of home. Allen pulled out her bag from the back and kissed her lightly as he handed it to her. "Are we a team, then?" he asked.

"Yes, a team," Dana replied. "A Jesus team."

Dana sat in Perry's office, which was small and simple, in the downtown headquarters. She told him she was interested in joining FISH full-time, and was pleased to find she would not only receive a salary slightly larger than her previous job, but benefits to match.

"I'm very happy you'll be joining us, Dana," Perry replied. "There is one 'catch.' We'll require you to use some of your salary to take college courses until you complete a degree."

Dana was crestfallen. She had loved the action and excitement of the group, but hadn't anticipated this.

Perry smiled sympathetically. "I get the feeling you're not keen on school. When we serve God, we must be prepared to take up our crosses. The assignments you've been on have been interesting and satisfying, but our work isn't always that way. There are long periods when we don't agree on an operation. When we finally do agree, it can take a long time for anything to happen. We have to be able to endure frustrations and disappointment.

"We want you to grow spiritually over time, and that includes living up to your potential. The specifics are different for each of us, but for you we think that means at least some more academic learning."

Dana promised she'd think and pray about it and let Perry know soon. As she started her old car, depression oozed around her heart. To go back to school seemed like such a burden, back to lectures, papers and tests. She didn't know if she could go through with it.

Her car approached the entrance for Lake City Christian College. A temporary sign announced a quilt exhibition in the gymnasium. Dana turned in and found a parking space.

A few persons moved about in the quiet, high-ceilinged gym arranged with antique coverlets on one side and freshly finished guild quilts on the other. Quilts hung from frames set up for their display.

Dana approached the first antique cover. The hand-sewn crazy quilt, intricately pieced, hung from brass rods. Multi-colored fabrics lay in logic-defying templates. No pattern, no form, thought Dana, but it is quite beautiful.

The next quilt repeated the shapes of a one-room school and an ink bottle with quill. Schoolhouse Quilt the card said.

Dana studied it. The little buildings looked uncomplicated. Intricate stitches formed the quill's feathers. For some reason, she thought of her of college entrance exams a few years ago. They were easy. It was this test she couldn't pass: What will you do with your life? Why can't you decide? She thought about how she admired Kathryn, and would enjoy learning from her. Maybe she could think in terms of one class at a time, one day at a time.

Close by, another coverlet was adorned with hundreds of needlepoint flowers, trees, golden birds. The card described three sisters who presented this quilt to their widowed mother. She imagined the patience and determination of those girls. Dana asked herself if she could maintain this kind of discipline.

Little as Dana Dushane knew about quilts, she recognized the next pattern of overlying circles. Double wedding ring. Would Allen Moran and she ever intersect so harmoniously? He so handsome, his green eyes set in an open, welcoming face. But she thought of their differences. He seemed so sure of his answers to life, and she still needed space and time for exploration.

The next quilt: squares surrounded by layers of rectangles on each side. Log cabin, another common pattern. How she had dreamed of moving from her apartment to a small home set near woods and a stream. Her secretary's salary had always prevented any real hopes.

She drifted through patterns and patchwork, fans, bowties, baskets of flowers. The modern quilts had freshly creative titles: Sailing on the Great Lakes; Tribute to Our Children; Wind-whipped Autumn. Millions of tiny stitches formed background patterns of infinite patience and care.

Was FISH finally the answer of what God wanted her to do with her life? Was it really the way to go?

Around a corner hung an unnamed coverlet. Apparently the organizers chose to give it a place in the show even though its origin was unclear. The quilt would remain anonymous, Dana realized, its Maker always mysterious.

Dana lost track of time admiring the quilted yellow-gold multi-faceted pattern called Rising Sun. It blazed in the glory of a light which penetrated her soul.

PART IV

CURTAINS

Ursa dodged the massive tombstones like a college halfback. The rising storm winds carried the stench of the half-man half-monster closing in upon her.

Ursa sensed the void of death. It was then she knew that when her life ceased, no consciousness would frame an existence for her. The soul was a figment of overly optimistic imaginations.

Dana slurped the last of her diet cola and crumpled the empty chip bag. By late Friday afternoon, Lake City Christian College was deserted by its otherwise eager early autumn students. But Dana hadn't felt like going home to cook for herself or do any of her plentiful homework. After a full week of classes, all she wanted was to relax.

Though the regular cafeteria was closed, there were plenty of machines to satisfy her junk food hunger. She sat at a corner table while the janitor emptied waste cans. He was now readying to mop, putting chairs on tables.

Guess I'll wait to see if the beast gets Ursa, Dana thought. Placing Lucia Lindell's popular thriller, *Curtains*, into her backpack, she headed toward the parking lot.

Near the front door of the building she saw Megan Wesley coming from an adjacent hall. Megan shared some classes with her and they were becoming friends. Megan's rounded features were set off by short hair the color of wheat.

"I finished *Curtains* last night," Megan said. "Don't read it alone."

"Don't tell me the end!" Dana cried. "I plan to be done with it tonight."

Dana did finish the book at a late hour. She didn't know which made her more edgy, the gruesome end of the thriller or the lack of nutritious food. Despite her mood, she readied for bed and turned off the lights. She was for once glad she lived in an apartment. Any monsters would have plenty of other people to distract them from her.

Nice going, Dana, she thought, to be so ready to sacrifice my fellow tenants.

The phone rang. The young woman's already anxious state increased several notches. No one called at this hour except with bad news. With trepidation she reached for the phone.

Megan Wesley's voice came loud and clear over the line. "You'll never guess!!"

"You scared me half to death. This better be good." Dana felt familiar enough with Megan to show her irritation.

"I'm sorry," Megan bubbled, un-deflated. "I told you not to finish the book alone. Anyway, I know you're as much of a Lucia Lindell fan as I am."

"Lucia Lindell? What about her?"

"She's coming to Lake City to live! I just got back from visiting my cousin. He's a real estate agent and said Lucia bought a mansion on the dunes. The old Frohley estate."

Dana hardly slept that night. Haunting visions of

beasts and cemeteries intertwined with thoughts of a famous author living almost next door.

Saturday morning's sunny crispness announced itself through Dana's loft-like bedroom. Though her apartment was narrow, the layout offered an upstairs and basement. She dressed and descended both stairs to heave her bike out of its storage. She mounted and pedaled to her 10:00 a.m. FISH meeting.

The members congregated in the downtown frame house which contained their offices. The former dining room served as conference area. Hardwood floor was covered with a patterned area rug large enough to contain the extra-long mahogany dining table and matching chairs. At an antique sideboard, Kathryn Tanis poured cider fresh from the morning farmer's market. Dana eagerly took a cup and sat contentedly.

She greeted Allen Moran with her usual ambivalence. How handsome he looked today in chinos and cotton shirt. How conservative, too, she thought. Therein lay a major problem of their relationship. She knew her opinions were usually more liberal, and she saw that as potential conflict. Allen and the others also grabbed cider and filled the rest of the table.

Perry Polk started the meeting with prayer.

"Father, we thank you for your many, many blessings. The bounty of our market today is only one example of the great variety of your goodness to us. May we humbly repay you by trying to obey your will."

Fuji Yamoto read minutes of the last meeting, most of which described reports of ongoing prayer projects.

Eben Stroud, the administrator, announced he had

spent some of the week doing paper work and some in his church project of building a new home for a low-income family.

Allen had ministered to people in the shelters and streets.

Jares Ranjah had caught up with personal business.

Kathryn and Dana were glad to have their first few weeks of school in, Kathryn as teacher and Dana as student.

Perry resumed. "Sounds like we're all pretty busy. Also, I have another item to add to our prayer list."

The members became more attentive.

"This city will be the new residence of Lucia Lindell, author of many best-selling thriller novels."

Dana saw Allen's expression change to disgust. The rest seemed either to have heard the news already or been able to take it more calmly.

"This will certainly upset the conservative community. There had already been numerous complaints to the administrator of Lake City High School, which carries her books in their library.

"We don't like the writing this woman does, with its glorification of evil and 'relative morality' philosophy. However, we don't know God's will here, so we're not going to pray against her coming to live in Lake City.

"At this point, we don't know if FISH is intended for any action concerning Lucia Lindell. But I feel her as a burden on my spirit. Therefore, I ask you all to pray about the situation this week and we will discuss the matter again next week."

With that, the meeting was adjourned. As the members left the building, Dana wondered what she would do the next meeting. She knew the FISH policy was to speak freely, but she wasn't sure she had the courage to tell them all that she read Lindell's books and didn't really see anything wrong with that. Perhaps she could start by telling Allen.

She yelled to him, already across the street at his truck. "Hey, Allen, you doing anything tonight? How about pizza?"

Surprised but pleased, he said, "6:30 OK? I'll pick you up."

"Then I'll pay the gas. I'd like to go to Paesano's in High Dunes."

She slipped onto her bike thinking, now I know why I should have started my homework last night.

High Dunes, a small town which lay about 15 miles north of Lake City, was more fishing town than touristy. Still, the scenery was beautiful this time of year. Dana wanted to use the extra driving time it took to get there to get her discussion 'over with.' Then perhaps she and Allen could enjoy their meal together.

She wasted no time and started almost as soon as they were out of the parking lot.

"Allen, I know you don't approve of Lucia Lindell, but I don't see what you have against her. Her books are entertainment. And all the critics acclaim her ability to evoke emotion."

Allen looked more pained than angry. "Which emotions? Hopelessness and despair? People read this stuff and then wonder why they are depressed."

"That's awfully strong. What about the adventure, the characters, the great prose?"

Allen shook his head. "St. Paul said, 'Whatsoever things are true, whatsoever things are honest, whatsoever things are just, whatsoever things are pure, whatsoever things are lovely, whatsoever things are of good report; if there be any virtue, and if there be any praise, think on these things. Those things, which ye have both learned, and received, and heard, and seen me, do: and the God of peace shall be with you.'

"Lucia Lindell, along with many other writers, glorifies destruction and hate. Her books are ghoulish, not to mention the explicit sex."

Dana retorted, "Aren't we given our brains to think and explore? People want to read about potential problems so they can decide what they would do in the same situations. They want to see where reason and ingenuity may take them."

Allen quickly responded. "And where is that? All I know is that the few times I've tried reading today's so-called great literature, I feel worse than joyless. Secular intellectuals connect melancholia with depth. They believe today's realism represents life. Well, people who don't believe in God are melancholy, all right, because they miss the fullness of God.

"If you do believe, it is an easy step to see that He created us to have free will, and the choice of purity gives us the best life. The modern problem is that people don't want to believe virtue is real. Certainly many act as though it isn't. Can't they see the pain and heartache, not to mention the disease, that impurity carries with it? Where is reason when it comes to denying this connection?

"When I read about Jesus, I sense being built up inside, in a way that lasts. The beauty of being God's child is being able to call on Him in any situation you find yourself. His help combines with our efforts in a creative, satisfying way. Isn't that what we are trying to do at

FISH?"

Dana stopped. She had to admit Allen had some good points. But she didn't find it as easy as he did to dismiss the value of secular literature. After a moment, she said, "I'll have to think about it. Let's enjoy the changing color of the leaves."

They couldn't help but appreciate the deep reds, golds and greens, of the forest. But the rest of the evening was undeniably strained, and they stuck to small talk through the pizza.

The Monday evening news announced the arrival of Lucia Lindell. A few enthusiastic reporters were shown trying to interview her at the airport.

"Miss Lindell, what made you choose Lake City?"

"Lucia, when's your next book coming out?"

A large male companion half-hid the stone-faced author as they quickly slid through the small terminal and outside to a long white limousine.

Lucia Lindell looked different than the publicity pictures Dana had seen. Her straight blond hair was longer now, she wore large glasses and was thinner, too. In her early fifties, she looked pale compared to those pert early photos.

The Frohley mansion can't be ready to live in, thought Dana. She tried to remember the turrets and bay windows of the rambling home. It had been boarded closed for many years. Lindell would have to keep writing best-sellers in order to afford the upkeep.

Though the season's change had started to shorten the days, Michigan's most westward inhabitants enjoyed more evening light than other Eastern Timers. Think I'll take a bike ride to the Frohley Estate, Dana decided. But I guess now we call it the Lindell Estate.

The young woman rode through Lake City's downtown and residential areas. She reached a road which ran along Lake Michigan and turned to an unpaved sand road which led through the wooded dunes. At a low point in the dunes, she got off and carried the mountain bike a distance from the trail. She was on public land, but hardly anyone came this way, still a distance from the beach-front parks. She laid the bike on its side and locked it.

Walking quietly west, she tried to justify her snooping by reasoning that writers, such as herself, had to be nosy to know what is going on.

No fence lined the estate. A clearing surrounded the brick buildings. The foundations lay sufficiently far from the Great Lake to avoid the inevitable erosion, but high enough for a magnificent view. Dana noticed a Mercedes parked near the barn-like garage, so she kept herself behind trees and bush as she rounded the estate's edges.

Standing in front of the house and looking up at the facade were Lucia Lindell and the man who had been with her at the airport.

In the still evening, the air carried their voices clearly.

"I'm offering those specialists from Chicago double their money if they can finish renovations in three weeks. I'll be staying with Helen until it's done. You can go back to New York."

"I don't like leaving you alone."

"Helen's a good friend. I won't be alone."

"I still say you can't run away from your problems."

"We've been through this. I'm not running." Then the best-selling writer laughed lifelessly. "Do I look like a halfback?"

Dana endured another long week of classes and studies. Once again, by Friday evening she could take no more. She didn't even feel like reading, so she called Megan. "Let's go out somewhere, anywhere."

Megan suggested a movie comedy she had been wanting to see. Afterwards, they stopped at the Coffee Cafe downtown to talk and have a snack. The cafe was almost empty. In one booth sat a man sipping coffee and reading a newspaper.

"Gerard!" Dana exclaimed. She introduced Megan to Gerard Conrad. He invited them to sit with him, which they gladly accepted. Megan first excused herself to the rest room.

"So how's lawyering these days?" Dana asked as she sat.

"How about I tell you over dinner tomorrow evening?"

Dana smiled and looked into Gerard's eyes. She had thought about him often in the months since last seeing him.

"I'll be ready by seven," Dana Dushane heard herself say.

Like before, Gerard provided an elegant backdrop for their conversation. This time they drove to High Dunes and ate at the Schooner, a restaurant situated on the channel connecting the small inland lake to Lake Michigan. Made of very aged wood, the building resembled a Spanish galleon. Top cuisine was served with low-key but consummate service.

Gerard had reserved a quiet corner by a window. Their hushed tones were safely private.

After both related their summer activities, which took them through the salad and into the main course, Gerard said, "I had a new client this week. Lucia Lindell."

Dana's eyes widened. "What was she like?"

"As interesting and mysterious as her books."

"You read her books?"

"Of course. I've never read anyone who delves into the questions of existence and relative moralities like Lindell."

"I agree. I'd love to meet her."

"I've read she's well received, even revered in the East Coast intellectual circles, but in my office she seemed pretty subdued--tired and distraught."

"I suppose it would be in poor taste for me to ask what Lucia wanted."

He smiled. "It probably would. She didn't ask me to keep it confidential, but I'm sure she wouldn't want the media to get a hold of it."

Dana could tell Gerard was bursting to tell her. "I promise it won't pass through these lips."

He glanced around and spoke even more quietly. "She asked me to make out her will."

Dana wanted to break her promise immediately and shout, Her will? Instead she formed a questioning look on her face.

Gerard read her expression easily enough. "I was pretty surprised myself. The woman's in town barely a week, not even moved into her new home."

"Maybe she's got a fatal illness."

"Why would she go to all the trouble of moving

1000 miles and renovating a run-down mansion?"

"The place *is* a mess." Dana looked sheepishly at the lawyer. "I, uh, happened to bike out there the other day."

Sure, Dana, his look said.

"Anyway, the bricks are disintegrating and some are gone. All the buildings need extensive tuck-pointing, and that's just the outside."

"I've never seen the place."

"It's pretty, Gerard. There are different colored bricks in patterns throughout the house and matching garage. The home is four stories, with several large chimneys. One whole corner is a huge turret with bent glass windows. I'm sure its top room would be perfect for writing," Dana finished wistfully.

"You know, there was something else. While Lucia was in my office she joked about the next book she planned. That it would be non-fiction, based on her own recurring dream. Something about seeing curtains torn from the top by an invisible force. It was an awkward moment."

Gerard sat back, having eaten the last bite. "I won't be needing dessert, but you go ahead if you like."

"No, I'd rather walk to the lighthouse by the channel."

The choppy water kaliedescoped the moon's reflected light. Gerard's warm presence protected her from autumn's first bitter winds. She turned toward him, and the lips which would not pass secret words touched his which had.

The intellectual crowd of Lake City was aflutter

from the moment they heard of Lucia Lindell's move. Before she even arrived, they contacted her through her local friend, Helen Rivera. Lindell accepted their proposal of a welcoming dinner and reception, and invitations were sent to the town's lists of art and cultural patrons. Among those on the receiving end was attorney Gerard Conrad. He called Dana to invite her as his guest, to which she excitedly agreed.

"I can't believe I'm going to that party!" Dana told a jealous Megan the next morning.

"I'd give my designer jeans to meet her," Megan sighed. "Some people have all the luck."

By the next Saturday morning FISH meeting, Dana drew up the courage to speak her mind. Perry started by prayer, and then added he had some traveling to do this weekend, so would keep the meeting short. He asked for comments and questions based on their last meeting.

Dana's heart pounded. She didn't like disagreeing with people, but knew she had to trust the members.

"I have to be honest," she started. "I read Lucia Lindell's books myself. They're entertaining and exciting. Of course, that's why she's on the best-seller lists. I guess I don't see how it hurts me to read them."

Dana glanced at the others. To her relief, no one acted shocked or judgmental.

Whenever Eben spoke, it was with his hands as well as his voice. The longer he talked, the more his arms rose and fell, as though he conducted his own expressions. He said, "A man may break his leg, which we consider bad. But maybe he did it while he was burglarizing a house. When he goes to the hospital to have it treated, he meets a chaplain who convinces him to change his ways. We consider this good, yet it might not have happened if he hadn't broken his leg from burglarizing.

"Lucia Lindell popularizes the notion of relative good and evil. She argues, in subtle ways, that there is no God, and there is really no one who can judge what is right or wrong."

Dana nodded, but was still skeptical. "I don't know the religion of every author for each book I want to read. Can't I stick to my own religion despite the writer's outlook?"

Dana continued. "It's just that sometimes I think people get a notion of what is right and wrong before they give something a chance. I've read some things that weren't about religion on the surface, but came through, in artistic ways, with beautiful feelings for God."

Eben twisted a pencil in his fingers when he listened. He answered, "As in every other aspect of our lives, we need to ask the Holy Spirit for guidance in each situation. He often shows us through our life experience."

Perry then cut in and said, "Thanks, Dana, for telling us how you honestly feel. As I said, I have to make this meeting short. How about you pursue the subject further with Eben after the meeting?"

Eben told Dana upon her inquiry that he'd be free on Friday, so they arranged for an in-house meeting.

Sunday afternoon, Allen called.

"Let's go out to the lake," he invited.

October's Indian Summer warmed the air. Colored leaves topped the dune cliffs along the lake line far into the hazy distance.

Allen and Dana walked one of the stone-lined breakwaters which projected hundreds of feet out into Lake

Michigan.   With small lighthouses on each end, they protected the channel of Lake City's inland lake.

The air cooled as they walked further from shore. Allen put his arm around Dana, and she felt an unusual peace. She felt different with Allen than with anyone else. He had a calming, almost stabilizing influence on her.

"I'm glad we haven't had any major FISH projects these last few weeks," Allen said. "I caught up on a lot of house repairs and other things."

"I know what you mean.   School's been pretty hectic."

When they reached the end of the breakwater, Allen asked Dana to sit on the edge with him. The waters were calm and the cement dry. A few other couples and families were out because of the beautiful weather, but did not linger. Several sailboats which had not yet been put to winter dry-dock decorated the sea.

Allen took her hand in his. "Dana, I want to tell you how I feel about you."

Seeing he was not joking, she turned her attention to him.

"I love you. I want to marry you."

Dana had to look away, to the water and sky, to determine if she had heard what she thought.

She turned back to his questioning face.   "Allen, there are so many subjects where we disagree. Besides that, you don't even know me."

She hesitated, not wanting to hurt him.   "I had a medical problem in my early teens. The only way it could be treated was by an operation. I'll never have my own children."

He gripped her hand more tightly.   "I don't care, Dana. Maybe we can adopt, maybe God wants us for other work. All I know is that I want to spend my life with you."

"I don't know what to say, except that I didn't expect this. You'll have to give me time to think."

"Of course." He kissed her lovingly and pulled her up with himself to the walkway.

Dana stared at the blackboard, uncomprehending. What interest could pre-calculus hold for her compared to the events in her life? If her mind wasn't re-living Allen's proposal, it was zooming ahead to the Thursday evening party for Lucia Lindell.

Dana knew she felt something for Allen, but she wasn't sure it was love. Then there was Gerard, who somehow seemed more exciting than Allen. The upcoming party was a perfect example. The elite of Lake City would be there.

Dana was wondering what she would wear when she noticed the other students putting away their books and papers. In semi-panic, she realized she missed the assignment.

Lord, thank you for friends, she silently prayed and scooted out the door in pursuit of Megan. They were heading toward the cafeteria and Dana invited her friend to join her for a snack.

When they sat down, Dana said, "This is embarrassing, but I missed the homework. What are we supposed to do?"

Megan smirked. "Thinking about your Lucia party? I shouldn't help you out."

Dana smiled, knowing her friend would. "I guess that's on my mind, but something else, too." She told the wide-eyed Megan about Allen's proposal.

"Wow! What are you going to do?" Megan asked.

"I truly don't know. I pray I make the right decision."

Dana went shopping that evening and found a straight, silk skirt in a soft ivory color. Dana was thrilled it had just been marked down. The dressy sweaters were all too expensive, but Dana knew just the one that would go with that skirt.

She drove to her parents' house on the south side of town. She wanted to tell her mother all the events in her life, anyway.

Dana's dad was at a meeting this evening, but her mother, Arie, was outside raking leaves. Dana grabbed the second rake and pitched in.

She told her mother about Allen. Arie stopped raking and scrutinized her daughter.

"So?" she asked.

"I don't know, Mother. I don't think I'm ready for marriage."

"It's a very big step. I'd like to see you done with school first." Arie rarely hesitated to let Dana know her thoughts.

"Anyway, mother," Dana changed the subject, "can I borrow your purple sequined sweater?" It was a pale cashmere with delicate sequined designs on front and back.

"If you tell me where you're going to wear it."

Dana did just that. She was so glad she and her mother wore the same size.

Gerard wore one of his Italian suits and looked especially sophisticated. The art museum annex was the site of the dinner reception. Fresh flowers decorated lace-covered tables.

A gushing, bejeweled chairperson greeted guests. Seats were not assigned, and Gerard and Dana sat a discrete distance back from the head table. All rose when Lucia Lindell arrived. Dressed splendidly, she projected confidence in an almost defiant manner. She was accompanied by another woman of about her same age.

Both sat at the head table. A luscious meal was served. Dana had never eaten such a delicate salad or succulent rolled roast. As they finished desert, the chairperson rose and stood at a small dais set up in the middle of their long table.

"We are so pleased to be honoring Ms. Lindell tonight. Before we ask her to say a few words, we'd like to present her with some thoughts of our own."

The city's newspaper publisher rambled about being a fan of Lucia Lindell from the very first book she put out and how he was on a list at the local bookstore to be called whenever her new thrillers arrived, etc. The Community Theater director talked of his plans to adapt her stories to the stage. The new mayor gave Lucia the keys to the city, a well-photographed scene.

Lindell seemed to take the fuss graciously. It was her turn to speak. The crowd hushed.

"How nice of you all to take such pains for this evening. I feel like you are friends already, especially since many of you are acquainted with Helen Rivera, my old (oops, sorry, Helen) college roommate with whom I am staying temporarily.

"I chose to come to Lake City to remove myself from the bustle of New York City, where I've lived all my life. I thought it was time for a change. Who knows, there may be a book in all this moving business."

The crowd reacted with light laughter.

"I write to experience my own consciousness. There are great vistas to be discovered, and I am happy to take the reader with me.

"I know this is a smaller town than what I am used to. Any town is smaller than New York. My atheism concerns some people. Already, some of Helen's friends have asked me, 'If you don't believe in God, where do you find your comfort?'

"I tell them I have no more to fear than they. In fact, I am better prepared to meet problems because I'm not under the delusion that a non-existent God will help me. I can evaluate my adversity, solve it, and move on with my life. Perhaps those people who question me never read my books."

Again, many in the audience chuckled.

"And so, I won't bore you with a long speech. Thank you again for this lovely reception. After we leave our seats, I'll be glad to stay and speak with you for a while longer."

She received a standing ovation. Since everyone then was already up, the room re-arranged itself into a line to meet with Lucia. Gerard had seen a lawyer colleague across the room, and took Dana to talk with him for a time. As the line shortened, Gerard and Dana made their way to speak with the author. Then Lindell shook their hands, and recognized Gerard as her lawyer. "Glad to see you again," she said to him, looking sincere. She told Dana she was glad to meet her, then turned to the next persons in line.

Dana could tell, from the alcohol on her breath and lines in her bloodshot eyes, that Ms. Lucia Lindell was not solving her own problems as well as she professed.

Eben answered the door and warmly hugged Dana. She was glad he took pains to put her at ease. Perhaps because he was the administrator and signed her check, she looked upon him as her direct boss, with Perry more the CEO. His warmth reminded her they were there for the Lord.

Eben had put a coffee pot and cups on a large tray, and brought them to one end of the dining room table.

"Thanks a lot for meeting with me," Dana said after they sat and prayed for God to grace them with understanding. He poured the decaf for her.

"I'm glad Perry suggested it."

"He is sure of where he stands about Lucia Lindell, but I'm not."

"Perry does try to be open-minded, but the initial feeling is hard to shake. I myself am more slow by nature to form opinions. I have to think a problem through before I know where I stand. I've read one of Lucia's books, and I think we have several problems.

"One has to do with her claim that the graphic horror and sexual scenes are meant to be metaphors, or literary substitutes, for her philosophies. Most conservative Christians would call it pornography.

"To be truthful, I don't think her books are on the best-seller list for their philosophies. She must know that many people buy them for the entertainment and titillation factors.

"Another problem is the philosophies themselves, such as relative morality and absence of life after death."

Dana interjected, "I'm wondering about the relative morality stuff, where things can be good sometimes and bad sometimes, or OK for one person and not another. Say like drinking wine. Christ changed water at the wedding in Cana to a fine wine. When he visited the common people and ate with them, I think He must have drunk wine with them, too. He used wine to pass to his disciples to use as a remembrance for his own precious blood.

"Yet we all know wine and other alcohol can be addictive and destructive in people's lives. People often drink it to get away from their problems, and it wreaks havoc in alcoholics' lives. Some Christians say we shouldn't drink wine at all."

Eben said, "The idea of no absolute right or wrong goes back a long way. Heraclitus was a Greek philosopher who lived 500 years before Christ was born. He and other thinkers of the time were grappling with concepts about God and the universe. He said the One, or their idea of God, was made up of diverse, opposing elements. In other words, if you didn't have the opposing elements, you wouldn't have God. Therefore, he said, right and wrong is only in the minds of people and not made up by God.

"The concept appears in other religions and theologies. The yin and yang of the far East; the modern view of conflict as tensions which are to be balanced within and between individuals."

Eben lifted and swung his left hand in arcs. "But the God of the Jews had very definite commands, and He wanted them followed. Obedience is a strong theme of the New Testament, also. Didn't the Father have a will for the Son? As phenomenal and mind-boggling as it is, I believe God has a plan, or at least His own desire in certain situations, for each human being. Some think that imposible, but the telephone and computer would have been thought impossible 200 years ago.

"The Bible gives us general principles to follow in

life's situations. For example, in Romans 14, Paul talks about persons who do not eat meat for religious reasons. He asks those who do eat meat to not eat it in the presence of those who don't, since "the kingdom of God is not meat and drink, but righteousness, and peace, and joy in the Holy Ghost.

"But when denominations, theologians and individual Christians disagree, what do we do? For years I wondered about the answer.

"As Perry and I worked on praying together, I read a book called *Touching the Invisible* by Norman Grubb. He described how his Protestant evangelical group came to learn how to seek God's will together. They talked about a particular problem honestly, and often when they started they disagreed.   Then they supplicated the Lord for guidance. They waited, and as time passed, they each felt God moving them toward conviction of a certain answer.

"The Catholic church is trying to find answers through pastoral councils, where lay members and priests share faith and pray together instead of arguing or voting on issues.

"These systems are similar to ours at FISH. We pray for spiritual protection and guidance, both for the other persons involved in the disagreement and ourselves. When we don't agree, we may just find that we ourselves hold some incorrect attitudes or thoughts.

"We at FISH seek souls more than doctrine, but I can't help thinking this system would help in obtaining any truth. We should be especially aware of that possibility when speaking with other Christians.   One must be courageous enough to hear the others out and realize we will be comforted by the Truth.

"When it comes to philosophical outlook, I believe

there are real sins and dangerous spiritual places. Secular authors and academic authorities, among many others, can be unconsciously tricked into believing a particular philosophy. They can't recognize their delusions, and in reality their mind-set drags them down into personal discomfort and eventually disaster."

Dana had finished her coffee and shifted back in her chair. She enjoyed watching Eben as well as listening. "But even when we try to follow God's commands, we fail," she said. "I know I've tried to help others and seem to make a mess of it. They get angry at me, or later I feel I've misrepresented God."

He smiled benignly. "The world is complex, and we can't figure God out. People *are* different and even Christians have honestly varying opinions of acceptable behavior. As individuals, it's often difficult to discern how is God guiding us, and to do a job in common even more factors are present. We get into our own minds what we think would help. It takes experience to discern well, even though it is a gift."

Eben reached to the sideboard and grabbed the copy of *Curtains* lying there. "I used to think I was alone in my distaste for novels, especially the classics. Then I read St. Augustine's *Confessions,* and I resonated with his dislike of investing emotions into people who aren't real.

"There is more to fiction than characters, though. We try to understand deeper truths. Unfortunately, many novelists either ignore God, disparage Him, or in my opinion grossly misrepresent Him. The question for me is, how many dark alleys and psychological dead ends are all that interesting?

"On the other hand, fiction can be Godly. It can bring aspects of creativity to the surface in a way that no other form is able. When I read, I try to discern which way a story is heading. Personally, I don't think it takes long to tell the tone, and if it is dark, I usually put it down."

Dana rose, saying, "I'd like to get back to LC's library. They close at four thirty on Fridays. Thanks, Eben, so much for the talk."

"My pleasure, certainly."

The days passed with a flurry. Every evening upon entering her apartment, Dana checked the answering machine. She was both glad and disappointed when it showed no messages. She was avoiding Allen because she didn't feel she could tell him what he wanted to hear. And she desired to go out with Gerard.

Maybe I'll call Gerard myself, Dana thought. After all, it's my turn.

She nervously punched the numbers for his home phone. He answered in a few rings.

"Gerard, hi. Have a few minutes?"

"Oh, Dana. Well, uh, I promised Lucia I'd help her pick out a boat."

"What? Lucia Lindell?"

"Yes, she came again to my office. Said she'd like to buy a cruiser for next summer, but would like me along, as her lawyer."

As her lawyer my sweat shirt, thought Dana. "I surely don't want to hold you up."

"Thanks. I'll get back with you later."

Later turned out to be the next week, after a long, lonely weekend. There wasn't even a FISH meeting, since Perry was still out of town.

It was Wednesday evening when Gerard finally

called. "Sorry I didn't get back with you sooner. Lucia wanted me to take the yacht out a few times before bad weather to make sure it worked OK. Did you eat yet?"

She hadn't, and they decided to meet downtown for fast food. Though after they hung up, Dana didn't feel much like eating. She went to the bathroom to spruce herself, but decided she wasn't any competition for the slim, sophisticated and very rich Lucia Lindell.

She met Gerard, already inside, then ordered only fries and a diet drink. The place was near empty and they sat in a back booth.

"I trust the yacht works well enough."

"Splendidly."

"I didn't know you are a yacht expert." Dana tried not to sound too snide.

"Dad had a cruiser. Of course, it wasn't the size of Lucia's. I used to have a speed boat, but my ex-wife sold it before our divorce."

"I suppose on your expeditions you got to know Lucia better."

Gerard nodded. "She's a fascinating woman. She trusts science to eventually explain everything, like human behavior. But she believes the scientists do not yet imagine the power and potentials of the human mind."

Dana half-heartedly tore some ketchup packets onto her fries. They lapsed into silence, starting to eat.

"Do you believe in God now, Gerard?" Dana asked.

Gerard cocked his head to one side, not expecting such a weighty question. "I'm not really sure. Since Corin's problem, I've been looking for deeper answers. The thing is, there are so many possibilities."

After a moment, Dana thought to ask, "Did Lucia mention her curtain dream again?"

"Yes. She's still getting the dream."

Dana said under her breath, "I guess Lake City wasn't far enough."

"What?"

"Oh, nothing."

"She described it to me a little more. The curtains are huge, and are made of cotton or linen with several dark colors. They're joined in the middle by gold clasps, so she can't see behind them. The most unusual part is the cherubs which are embroidered into them. They must be fantastic-- she said she's never seen anything like them in real life.

"Then the curtains start tearing from the top. She gets such a terrified feeling that she wakes up before they are torn even half way. She said there is something very powerful behind them, but doesn't know what."

"I really think Lucia is not able to face her fears like she says. That's why she made out her will."

He breathed deeply. "Lucia told me that although she herself is not taken up with the occult, many of her fans are. They belong to Satanic or witchcraft groups. They have a fascination with her and some of them get aggressive when she ignores either their repeated invitations or they themselves on the streets. They've given security a rough time, and Lucia was unable to walk from her apartment building anymore. Apparently, the last time she did, they shouted threats about curses and even death."

Dana realized this situation was probably the 'running away' to which Lucia's male friend referred. Dana shook her head, wishing she could say something profound.

She said instead, "Not to change the subject, but would you like to come to LC's theater next week? The students are putting on their first play of the year."

Gerard did not respond immediately. "I'll have to

check my calendar. Can I get back with you?"

"Of course. Leave a message if I'm not there."

Dana could tell Gerard was putting her off. She didn't say much more except "goodbye" at the end of the meal. Driving home, Dana started to wonder if she should break her promise of silence and tell FISH members what she knew about Lucia. Was the author in immanent danger from one or more of her fans? Dana knew she'd feel responsible if anything happened.

The next day, between instructions of math, science and religion, Dana thought about Allen. She knew she'd have to face him at the next FISH meeting. She also realized what a dear he was being for not calling, since he must be wondering what's going on in her mind. She decided to ask him to come for dinner at her apartment.

Dana wasn't much for cooking, and she figured Allen should know about that first hand. Also, she liked weird things like kumquats and baked eggplants. At least healthy food balanced the junk food she also liked.

He seemed happy to accept. She prepared an easy dish of chicken and rice baked with mushroom soup. She also resorted to a can of green beans to make the vegetable as easy as possible.

Allen came at the appointed time. Dana had forgotten how good she could feel with him. Gerard's behavior only reinforced her appreciation of Allen's reliability.

The chicken needed a few more minutes. She gave him a soft drink and they sat in the small living room.

"Thanks," she said, "for giving me time and space to think."

"You're welcome. Gilbert and I wouldn't want to rush you."

"You know we have a lot of differences, Allen. Take the environment. Every time I see a tree cut down I get upset. I love nature, and see it as a way to appreciate God's creativity. You look at the human aspects of business and economic growth, which I can understand, but you seem to think the environment will take care of itself.

"Another example. You think our cultural problems can be legislated away by government, where I see the answer in church-oriented grass roots projects."

Allen nodded. "Yes, we have differences. I know where I stand, and I want others to know, too. I like having my life clear-cut, but I also want to learn."

He got up and sat next to Dana on the sofa, facing her. He put his hands on her arms, and moved them softly up to her shoulders. Those hands had the power to melt her tensions. "But to me, the most important thing is love. If we love, we can work things out. And I do love you," Allen said, and kissed her, longer this time.

"I think I like being loved by you," Dana replied.

Friday morning at 8:30, Dana drove to LC's to wait for her first class. She walked through the long, glass-lined corridors and sat on a cushioned bench outside the room, still in session with an 8:00 advanced Christian Ed. taught by Kathryn Tanis.

Dana hadn't had any of Kathryn's classes yet, but she liked to listen to her talk. A lilting voice emitted sound waves carrying the facts of physics, chemistry and biology to the back of the room and beyond. Today she mentioned a test, and seemed to be reviewing.

"Remember, class, the body, mind and soul form a complex which interacts intricately. This complex absorbs input, it processes that input. Those processes cause changes within the complex. However minute the individual changes are, they are significant to body, mind and soul. Accumulated, the input affects our personalities and health, our outlooks and perceptions.

"God promises us the precious gift of Divine Nature, through knowledge of Jesus Christ. We desire to be receptive to God's system..."

Someone interrupted Kathryn with a question about the upcoming test. Dana replayed the teacher's words in her own mind, and rearranged them with the very processes to which Kathryn referred.

Input is very important. Input can alter us. The content of Lucia Lindell's books that so repulsed Allen-- what changes in body, mind and soul did that cause?

Dana took a deep breath and realized some input can't be helped. But then again, some can.

That evening, Dana poured herself an orange juice, put on her sweats and snuggled into her stuffed chair. She picked up the King James Bible, given to her by her family when she was confirmed. Since Allen liked to quote this version so much, she figured she'd use what she already had. She found the prose difficult to understand sometimes, but it did have a poetic ring.

Dana had read parts of the Bible before, but now wanted to cover front to back. She sped through Creation, Noah's flood, the Tower of Babel, and the destruction of Sodom and Gomorrah. She recognized great names of old: Abraham and Sarah, Isaac, Jacob and Leah, Joseph, Moses.

The stories were quite interesting and reading went quickly until she passed the ten commandments and ran into all the laws for the people of Israel.

The laws were interesting in a sense: one could picture how a Hebrew servant who was purchased and worked for six years would feel when, on the seventh year, he would be allowed to 'go out free for nothing.' But Dana was getting pretty tired, and the rules on the pages started blurring. Then God started telling Moses how to build the temple.

> *And they shall make an ark of shittim wood: two cubits and a half shall be the length thereof, and a cubit and a half the breadth thereof, and a cubit and a half the height thereof.*

Surely I'll be better able to appreciate this in the morning, Dana thought.

Oh, well, one more chapter. Exodus 26.

> *Moreover thou shalt make the tabernacle with ten curtains of fine twined linen, and blue, and purple, and scarlet: with cherubims of cunning work shalt thou make them.*
>
> *The length of one curtain shall be eight and twenty cubits, and the breadth of one curtain four cubits: and every one of the curtains shall have one measure.*
>
> *The five curtains shall be coupled together one to another; and other five curtains shall be coupled on to another.*
>
> *And thou shalt make the loops of blue upon the edge of one curtain from the*

selvedge in the coupling; and likewise shalt thou make in the uttermost edge of another curtain, in the coupling of the second.

Fifty loops shalt thou make in the one curtain, and fifty loops shalt thou make in the edge of the curtain that is in the coupling of the second; that the loops may take hold one of another.

And thou shalt make fifty taches of gold, and couple the curtains together with the taches; and it shall be one tabernacle.

The young woman didn't feel her tiredness anymore. She read the verses twice, three times. Each time she was struck how closely they matched the description.

Dana spoke her wonder out loud. "Could these be Lucia Lindell's curtains?"

It was Saturday again. Dana had taken a few tests in her classes at LC's that week and felt relieved they were done. She enjoyed greeting the FISH members, realizing she had missed them in the passage of two weeks.

They started right in on discussing and praying about the community and other ongoing concerns. Lucia Lindell was on their list.

"Anything new on Lucia?" Perry asked.

Through the week, Dana had internally debated whether to break her promise to Gerard and tell FISH members about Lucia's will, her dreams and her dangerous fans. She knew they would keep it confidential, but she kept remembering about sealing her lips. She prayed daily for the author's safety.

"I guess we will continue to keep her on our potential projects list for a while," Perry decided. "I have some conviction and burden about her, but it's just not taking any form."

Dana noticed an energy growing within her. She started to feel weakened, almost unable to move, but in a relaxed way. It was like every muscle fiber was being individually warmed.

As the others prayed, Dana felt she was receiving a directive from God to keep Lucia's secrets.

Sunday after church, Dana called Gerard. She again asked him if he had time to speak.

"A few minutes. I'm afraid I do have some plans this afternoon."

"I understand, Gerard. I just want to tell you about something I came across." She read him the verses from Exodus.   "These tabernacle curtains match Lucia's descriptions perfectly!"

"Well, I don't know. It seems unlikely."

Dana deflated. "Could you at least tell her about them?"

"I don't want her to know I told anyone else."

"Well, tell her you remembered about it from Sunday School days and looked it up again. You're a lawyer, think of something."

"Fine, well, I've got to get going. Thanks for your concern."

Dana hung up the phone in frustration. She channeled her energy to prayer. Lord, let him at least tell Lucia about the description.

Dana was also depressed by Gerard's attitude. She

was sure he was on his way to visit Lucia.

Dana pondered about the similarity of the Jewish desert tabernacle with the later temple built in Jerusalem. She got out her Bible and turned to the New Testament. She found the place where Jesus died in St. Mark .

> *And Jesus cried with a loud voice and gave up the ghost. And the veil of the temple was rent in twain from the top to the bottom. And the centurion, which stood over against him, saw that he so cried out, and gave up the ghost, he said, Truly this man was the Son of God.*

Dana shuddered. How angry the Father must have been when mankind killed his Son. He ripped the very curtain of the Holy Inner Sanctum. She put the Bible back down.

The day was too nice to stay inside, but Dana had more homework. She gathered her books and put them in a pack. The college campus was only a mile and a half from her place, so she walked as she often did.

Leaves were still falling. Dana reflected on her life with the Lord. She knew she wanted to live her life well, but there were so many temptations, more than she had realized. On the other hand, though following Christ could be difficult, there was absolutely nothing like it.

Dana took a sweeping look at the scenery before entering the college. She walked into the library and got down to studying.

Through the long weekday evenings, Gerard didn't

call. The cold, chilly rain kept Dana inside and irritable. But Saturday morning dawned on a lovely, crisp day. Dana rode her bike the few miles to the FISH headquarters. It was time for another meeting.

Perry started the FISH projects with Lucia Lindell. "I feel we're not finding the way to pray for her, or any ideas on what to do. I recommend we take her off our list. As usual, we'll put her on the long-term roster."

He referred to a list made of persons in need of prayer, but not active FISH projects. Church volunteers, many of them retired persons, prayed for them for a period of time.

The group agreed. Dana didn't understand why, but she felt relief. God had brought Lucia into her own life, and only He knew the reason.

"One other thing," Perry said, with a nod toward Dana and Allen. "I think its about time we got to the initiation rites."

Ranjah said, "I will arrange."

Eventually, the meeting was adjourned. Allen saw Dana mounting her bike and said, "Looks like fun."

"It is. You have one?"

"No, maybe you'd like to help me pick one out sometime. Want to ride over to my place? I'll make you lunch."

"Sounds good. I'd like to cover a few miles first."

"Take your time."

Lucia's mansion filtered into Dana's thoughts. She decided to see how the work was coming. She left the road at the same spot as before, and again laid down the bike and locked it. She looked around. Since the rain, the leaves were almost all down. She had to stay further away to be inconspicuous, but clearly saw a moving van backed up to the rear entrance of the house.

No people were immediately in sight, so she came a little closer. The home's brickwork had obviously been completed. The sharpness of the bricks edges cut into the background sloping dunes. Shades had been precisely matched, and the building was indeed a reminder of the masterwork of nineteenth century architecture and construction.

Dana wondered what was happening inside. She stood immobile for a few minutes, but didn't want to keep Allen waiting. She returned to the bike with a perplexing sinking feeling.

The sight of Allen's cute bungalow cheered Dana. It had a back mud-room, and Dana carried the bike inside the unlocked door.

"I'm here," she announced.

Allen was in the kitchen. "I got ambitious, making my famous meatballs and spaghetti. Wanted you to try it. I heated some cider with cinnamon. Take it into the living room."

Though Dana had a good workout, the wind had been cold. She was happy for the warm drink and cozy atmosphere. She hadn't visited Allen's home all that often, so looked around in curiosity.

The TV was small but the radio was large and stereo. She flipped it on.

The unique sound of Christian rock blasted forth. Dana turned down the volume and, after stretching her muscles a bit, sat back on an Afghan-covered couch.

The curtains of Lucia's vision protruded onto her mind. She wanted to get Allen's opinion without sounding suspicious. But that would be about impossible.

Allen came in with his own cider. "Sauce needs a few more minutes."

"That's fine," Dana reassured. "I didn't expect you to go to all this trouble. Oh, it smells delicious."

He sat on a chair opposite the couch.

"I've been thinking," she said.

"I hope so."

She decided on the directly indirect approach. "I'd like your opinion of something, but you can't ask me why."

"Sounds interesting."

"What do you think about the curtains tearing in the temple after Christ died on the cross?"

Allen looked at her with an odd expression. "What do I think of them?"

"Right."

"Well, let's see. The Israelites in the desert on the way from Egypt to the Holy Land built a tent-like tabernacle for God. Then Solomon raised a great temple in Jerusalem of the same specifications.

When Babylon captured Jerusalem, the temple was burned. But the Jewish people returned and rebuilt it, which is described in the book of Ezra.

"Before Christ, our Father let Himself be worshiped in a small area of the temple, the Holy of Holies. Not that He had to be contained in one place, but in a sense He was contained to one tribe of people.

"Once His Son died, the victory against death on earth was won. It's kind of like God opened Himself to the world after that, through His Son."

Dana thought about Allen's words. She hadn't considered the symbolic aspect of the curtains.

"You know Allen, you're pretty special."

"All God's children are."

The spaghetti was ready and turned out to be wonderful. Dana discovered the advantages to a guy who can cook.

While they ate, she asked Allen, "Do you have any doubts about joining FISH?"

"No. I'm pretty convinced it's what God wants for me. What about you? What about your writing?"

"After I'm done with school I'll have plenty of time to write."

"It will be fun to work together."

"You know, I think you are right."

On Dana's bike ride back to her apartment, her thoughts turned once again to Lucia Lindell. The woman saw the curtains ripping apart in her dreams, but always woke in terror before knowing what was behind them.

If Lucia wouldn't be so scared, Dana reflected, she could bask in the love of the God who opened Himself to all.

Sunday evening, Dana wracked her brain for an excuse to call Gerard. Maybe he was busy with work all week, she reasoned, unconvinced.

She picked up the phone and asked herself, why not try the truth? When he answered, she said, "Hi, Gerard. I wondered if you told Lucia about the curtains."

"I promised you I would and I did." He sounded testy.

"What did she think?" Dana asked meekly.

"She doesn't believe her dreams have anything to do

with the Bible. You know she just wrote a book called *Curtains* and it was after publication that her vision started.

"She said as the curtains tear in half, her inner self is telling her about the two levels that her writing is taking, one being the entertainment aspect and the other the literary. She feels subconsciously she is afraid to release her own full powers."

Incredulous, Dana's mind spun. The only levels in question were the dry, joyless inner life Lucia was leading as compared with the potential to answer God's call of spiritual growth.

Before she could respond, Gerard said, "Dana, I know you would want me to be honest. Lucia and I are involved in a physical relationship."

Dana knew Gerard was becoming distant, but these words stung. "I think it best we don't see each other," she managed to say.

"I agree. Sorry for any bad feelings. Goodbye then."

"Goodbye," she could hardly say before he hung up.

Dana's thoughts flowed much hotter than her words had. Yes, I would want you to be honest, Gerard. I would also want you to not be sleeping with Lucia.

Her vitriol was not confined to Gerard. How could Lucia ignore the description of the curtains in the Bible? How could she so boldly deny her obvious anxieties and inability to overcome them? The philosophies Lindell so proudly advanced did little to assuage the terror she felt from her odd fans and the dream visions.

It was late. It had taken all evening for Dana to gather the courage to call Gerard, and now she felt spent. She readied for bed, her anger starting to be replaced by the hurt of Gerard's rejection.

Monday and Tuesday, Dana intermittently fretted over her dealings with Lucia. Maybe she could talk with her, reason with her. Maybe she should tell the FISH members after all.

Tuesday evening, she flipped on the local news. She was preparing supper, but when she heard the newscaster say, "Lucia Lindell..." she quickly dropped her utensils and watched alertly. "... is the object of a lawsuit by State Citizens for Cultural Decency. They will be suing the school systems which carry her book, and Lindell's publishers for distributing pornography to minors."

A picture of Lucia glared in the background. "Ms. Lindell's lawyer, Gerard Conrad, says she will take no interviews and speak only through him.

"In other state news..."

So much for arranging to talk with Lucia, Dana thought. She turned off the TV. Lucia had more problems, and FISH couldn't help her with them. No more than they could provide indefinite protection from her kooky fans.

Dana remembered a passage she read in the FISH manual. 'You can't force people's minds. You plant a seed, pray it grows. Ultimately, the decision is theirs.'

Dana sighed. Lucia may come to know our Lord, or may never. Only God could straighten out Lucia's life, and right now she was rejecting Him.

Dana was recovering from Gerard's behavior. She realized she nursed another pain, from Lucia's refusal to let God into her life. If it feels so bad to me, Dana thought, I wonder how He feels.

But the pain was burning off to a sanctifying peace. Dana felt she couldn't do more. God allows people the free will to choose, Dana reflected, and so must I.

In bed that night, in the darkness, Dana pictured the

great temple curtains. She believed, in a way, the vision
was meant for herself as much as Lucia. From behind those
deep-toned drapes, with cherubims gloriously embroidered,
the love, the love, came pouring forth.

After classes Wednesday, Dana drove to Allen's
house. She was happy to see his car in the drive and pulled
in behind it.

He was surprised to see her at the door.

"Have coffee on?" she asked.

"No, but I'll make some."

She sat at the kitchen table. How her life had
changed in the last few months.

After Allen filled the cups and sat with her, Dana
took his hand and looked in his eyes.

"I wanted to know, is the offer still good?"

Allen seemed to understand what she meant, but
asked, "What offer?"

"Your offer to marry me."

He put his free hand on top of hers.

"That will always be good."

"Allen, I love you. I want to wait for a while, but I
accept."

Allen drove Dana in his pick-up to the monastery by
the great lake. Though trees were now bare, the late
chrysanthemums softened the stone fence of the monastery
with color. Dana could see the stucco steeple arising from
the lower gray stone sanctuary. The walkways which had
been covered with snow in April now twisted undisturbed
around the buildings and through the wooded dunes.

They entered the church and walked down the center isle. The heavy oak pews were plain, but well crafted.

The other FISH members sat in front. Then a priest entered, and Perry, Allen and Dana walked to the altar.

The priest stood before Perry Polk, who placed a vestment around the inductees' necks. The three knelt before the priest.

"In the name of the Father, the Son and the Holy Ghost, Amen," the priest spoke in a low voice. *"*I will go unto the altar of God."

The three answered, "To God, the joy of my youth."

The priest said, "Most blessed Jesus Christ our Savior, with the living Holy Ghost, we supplicate to You and ask the Mercy of the Lord God, Creator. May the Almighty and merciful Lord grant us pardon, absolution, and full remission of our sins.

"Saints, angels, sisters and brothers gathered here, pray to the Lord our God for these newly anointed members."

He dipped his finger in holy oil and drew a cross on their foreheads. Then he put his hands on the inductees heads.

"The Word is the True Sword. May Dana Dushane and Allen Moran learn to carry this Sword in the service of the Almighty God, Three in One."

The FISH members stood. An inner song arose within Dana Dushane, humming and cascading.

The priest said, *"*O Lord, hear my prayer."

She and the other members responded, "Let us do Your special bidding, Your servants who live by 'Faith, Inspiration, Service & Hope.'"

PART V

THE WRITER

While standing at the counter, Evvie Burke noticed a man through the large windows at the Michigan Secretary of State's office. He stood in a corner of the sidewalk created by the square entryway to the building. The recent snow was yet unshoveled there, making it an unusual place to be loitering. A wide-brimmed hat obstructed his face, all but the beard from which his cigarette protruded. The clerk saw him toss something to the ground before he left.

Those bums think they can toss their junk anywhere, Evvie huffed to herself. Before leaving for the weekend, she left a note to the janitor who came later that evening. Evvie had a personal pride in the building where she worked, and felt satisfaction upon its neat appearance.

Julie Greene worked at night as janitor at the SOS in order to support her baby while she studied toward a degree in business. She saw Evvie's note and came to the front of the building. She knelt and saw a concentrated cranberry juice can sitting on top of the snow. She grabbed it firmly.

After the detonation, Julie was thrown twenty feet. She was knocked immediately unconscious before having time to realize she'd never reach for anything with her natural right hand again.

Dana Dushane stopped on her way from an early Saturday morning college class to pick up a few groceries and the local newspaper. Though Dana was organized in many segments of her life, a weekly grocery shopping plan was not one of her natural capabilities. In fact, the job seemed to evade any discipline she tried to force upon it. She could only manage buying for a few days, or sometimes a meal, at a time.

One of the few neighborhood stores which survived the ravenous competition of convenience gas stations stood on a corner between the school and her dwelling. All her needs, however limited in selection, lay stocked within its old-fashioned shelves and coolers.

Dana thanked God for her job with FISH, paid for the groceries and put them in the car before approaching an outdoor paper machine. The glare on the front glass had kept her from seeing it before. EXPLOSION AT SOS MAIMS WOMAN. Dana gasped. She had worked at one of the centers several years and knew most of the employees. Quickly she got to the car and read further. It was a young single mother named Julie Greene. Her right arm had been amputated above the elbow. Dana realized Julie had started working at that office after Dana had already left the SOS.

In Dana's emotional state, she had no desire to read the rest of the paper. She threw it in with the brown bags and drove home.

On the way into her apartment, she scooped her mail out of the box. A letter from a publisher peeked through the rest. Dana had found time to write a story over the holidays and send it in. She went inside excitedly to read their reply. She fantasized as she quickly put away milk and frozen juice.

"Superb!" it would read. "Exciting and well-paced,

poignant yet upbeat. Profound, but readable, your novel rends the heart. Simply brilliant in putting teenagers in touch with their spiritual selves."

"We, Puberty Publishers, will pay any amount to get your contract. We will print more books, sign more contracts, more, more, more."

Dana Dushane sighed. She opened the envelope and read what the contents actually said. It was a form letter. "Purity Press does not have need at this time for your material. Thank you."

She tossed it into a box in the corner of her small apartment. Failure to recycle my rejection slips could cause a worldwide depletion of writing material, she cynically thought.

Dana's parents had been ecstatic when she told them she'd decided to go to college, but they didn't quite understand her evasive explanation of her new job at FISH. Dana reflected that there's probably always some problem in human relationships. When one gets worked out another takes its place.

Dana called the hospitals to find Julie Greene's address. She could at least use what writing skills she had to send the poor woman a card of encouragement. Dana thanked the Lord Julie hadn't lost both arms. Imagine not being able to touch your baby's face with your own hand. She finally found the room number among one of the city's three hospitals.

Staring at the phone in a depressed state, she called Allen's number. His voice, in just a simple 'Hello,' was soothing to her nerves.

"I'm never going to be published," she forcefully lamented.

"Now, Dana. You tell me yourself how difficult it

is and how persistent you have to be."

"My stories are too boring."

"Why?"

"I think it's because I'm afraid to write a uniquely sinister plot that will give some jerk or jerks ideas to do it him-/her-, or themselves. You know, like the bomber of the federal building in Oklahoma was said to have gotten his idea from a novel."

"I've always thought real-life stories of people coming to Christ and of what God does for us are always more interesting than made-up ones. I admit Christian culture needs good fiction too, but you don't even need to be an author. You have your job with FISH."

"Well, I think God created people to be creative," Dana groused. "Besides, FISH might not be around forever."

"I will, though," Allen teased. "I don't mean to cut you off, but I've got to get going. I have an appointment."

"Oh, I'm sorry Allen, I should have asked if you had time to talk."

"No problem. The dentist. You can write about my courage going there."

Feeling very *dis*couraged, Dana knew she had to do something. No use lying on the faded sofa and mulling over her story's lost hope of movie rights. The gray cold day would beat her unless she joined it.

I'll go skiing, Dana decided. She quickly brushed her chestnut hair and donned her wool sweater.

Dana had participated in various school sports and considered herself modestly athletic. She loaded her car with battle-scarred equipment and drove ten miles from her place in Lake City to a Michigan state park with cross-country skiing paths. The road led west along the shore of Lake City's large inland lake, then turned north to follow Lake Michigan's coast. In winter, the great lake's waves froze in layers and, pushed by more waves, formed dunes of ice to face the ancient sand hills on the other side of the shore.

She pulled into the state park, then attached her skis at the car. She slid through tall pines heavy laden with snow. The daylight would last about another hour. Dana liked the simple lodge that had a fireplace and rental equipment, but there was no reason for her to enter. She saw several sets of adults and children who busied themselves in various stages of choosing, removing or attempting to attach themselves to skis. Dana chuckled at the sight and fluently glided by.

She skied to a cross-road, and through the leafless brush and sparse pine noticed a single skier going up one of the hills. He stopped at a tree with a split trunk along the trail, put something in the woody hole then pushed on until out of sight.

Curiosity moved the young woman toward the tree. A paper was tucked inside. Dana strained to see if anyone was watching, then took the paper and put it in her pocket. She planned to circle to put it back. A stand of pines at a curve in the trail provided a protected spot to unfold the note. It read, "End of the World, 1/29, 8 pm."

Dana took a sharp breath, refolded the paper quickly and rushed back to replace it into the trunk. Skiing as well as possible on weak knees back to the lodge area, she was just in time to see the same man enter his vehicle. She threw her snow-covered gear into her car and took the turn he did, trying to stay a distance behind him.

Her writer's mind was working overtime. Was this man a spy? A religious fanatic? Maybe he was pathologically depressed and planned to commit suicide.

The headlines of the day's paper came to her mind. Could he be a terrorist? Was his group placing a bomb somewhere in their unsuspecting city? Jan. 29 was not very far away. Two weeks.

His olive jeep turned off the main thoroughfare into a run-down neighborhood. No cars ran between them now, so she slunk down in the seat as far as she could. The narrow street allowed no parking, and her tires scraped the sidewalk curb several times.

Great, Dana, she said to herself. Nice and subtle.

He turned a corner, then parked behind a long-unpainted, seedy building, got out and went inside. Dana hadn't pictured this man as the seedy-building type.

She tried to describe him to herself: pretty intelligent, good-looking, and, well, unseedy. No wonder nobody buys my writing, thought Dana.

The secretary took her car to a parking space a small distance from the house, and hunched down again. She locked all the doors, tried to keep warm with short bouncy muscular efforts and marveled at how ridiculous she felt.

She would have left within two minutes, except that an old pickup truck pulled in front of the house. A middle-aged man with hunting cap got out and went inside.

Dana believed herself to be freezing to death. She breathed a sigh of relief when her car started--she'd hate to get stranded here.

There was nothing to do. She couldn't very well call the police because of one slip of paper. She went home and tried to forget about it, but didn't sleep and carried it with her the next day.

Dana was distracted in church and hardly heard the sermon.   In the afternoon, she headed toward FISH headquarters.   Both Dana and Kathryn Tanis had been relegated to Saturday morning classes at Lake City Community College this semester, so the FISH meetings had been rescheduled from regular Saturday mornings to a variety of times.   This week happened to be Sunday afternoon and Dana had never been so glad to have a FISH meeting.

Allen was already sitting at the table and gave her a big smile.

He is *so* cute, Dana sighed.   To him she said, "Looks like the dentist did a good job on you."

He laughed.   "I'm just trying to promote my upcoming lecture at Bayside Baptist Church.   Here's my brochure."

She looked at it. *Preparing for the End Times,* a presentation by Pastor Allen Moran. January 18, 8 pm.

"What's wrong, Dana?" Allen asked.   "You look pale."

"Oh, nothing, nothing.   Just have a little bug maybe."

They all sat down.   As Perry was opening with prayer, Dana wondered about this eerie coincidence.   Was there any possibility of Allen being involved in whatever she had witnessed?   But, she decided, this was not a matter to keep to herself.   She needed the help of the FISH members.

"I think our first item on the agenda is the bomb which went off at the SOS yesterday," Perry stated.

They all nodded.

"Did you know the person who was hurt, Dana?" Perry asked.

"No, she came after I left. Hasn't been there more than a month."

He shook his head. "What a shame. Anybody know anything about it? How about you, Allen? You're out on the street a lot."

"I'll see what I can find out. And I'll keep my eyes and ears open."

Dana said, "I don't know if this has anything to do with the bombing, but..." She went on to describe her skiing experience.

No one knew any other connection, but they prayed a long time for God's guidance. Most there felt a strong conviction that there was something God wanted them to do.

Allen's seminar was Tuesday evening. The church was cool and dark. A great dove, illuminated by alter candles, was suspended above Allen, evoking in Dana a feeling of protective affection. As he began, he seemed to waver but became steadier as he continued. "I won't really talk about the End Times," he said. "I want to talk about being ready for them. About knowing God is real, and how that should make a difference in the way we live."

He spoke fairly quietly. He was not the dynamic speaker that her own Pastor Schick was. Still, Dana was glowing. It was miraculous to be there, to be loved by the man who was up there, who in turn was so assured in his love from God.

Why couldn't she be trusting? She couldn't drop the matter of the paper in the tree, how close the words came to the subject he was now addressing. Yet he seemed to be steering away from the details of the End Times and leading into the present and our responsibilities now.

A glitter of light was reflected from Allen's neck. She smiled about his pet pewter fish Gilbert and how he kept him always near his chest.

The crowd of about 30 people seemed to enjoy his talk and engaged him in discussion afterwards. Before the talk, Allen had asked her to meet him when done for a snack at a nearby diner. She waved to him and left, knowing he'd leave when he could. Though it was a few blocks, she drove because of the icy pavements. On the way, she turned on her car radio.

"Yesterday, in the Manistee National Forest," the reporter announced, "a lone hunter stepped on a land mine covered by snow. He was found this morning, dead from blood loss and exposure to cold temperatures. The explosive was a plastic 'smart' mine. This is the self-disabling type, which indicates it was buried within the last 48 hours.

When Allen arrived at the restaurant, Dana told him the news. "It was near a town about 100 miles north of here," she said.

"Man." He looked at her with troubled eyes. Dana returned eye contact. His, the color of pine woods, were so intense that she wanted to reassure him. But what was on his mind?"

He said, "I don't know who lives in the house you saw, but when you described the man with the hunting cap he reminded me of a prisoner I was jail ministering to--I'll call him 'Joe.' He had gone broke, he claimed, because the government over-regulated his business. He had done some property damage to an inspector's car and refused to pay the fine and restitution. Joe belonged to a militia group which meets up north, but he told me he was going to drop out. He came to my place a few times after he was released. That's when I saw him wear the hunting cap. I think he could tell I was sympathetic."

Dana choked out, "Sympathetic?"

"Joe served his time. He seemed like a regular guy who just had so many problems he couldn't handle them. The government came along and it was the last straw. I was hoping I could help him get a job, put his life back together. He talked a lot about hunting, then one day said he was moving north. I keep thinking of him, but I can't believe it could be him."

Allen pulled his gaze away from Dana and stared into his coffee.

"But," he mumbled, "you never know how Satan and his demons will twist a person's thoughts."

Dana said, "Not everyone believes that."

"I think it's because science doesn't understand how demons can work that we pretend they are not there.

"Certain things have struck me about our culture. If we talk about evolution being survival of the fittest, there are parts of our behavior, as I see it, which don't fit into the pattern. Since men have been in charge of most law-making, why has marriage become part of our legal system? According to evolutionists, women are the ones who want the security of monogamy.

"Even though many women now are raising children alone, no one can deny the hurt they all bear when the father is not present. I believe it is the church, and therefore God, who gave us the ideal of marriage so strongly because it *is* the best and most loving way to raise children.

"And think about our society. Sheer acquisition might be a survival trait, but what about fads? Why do they get started and spread? Why did so many people want a certain kind of furniture in the fifties and then decide it was ugly in the seventies? Why do teenagers wear styles of hair and clothes they must have one year and wouldn't be caught dead in the next?

"These fickle traits strike me as spiritual, just as virtue and love are spiritual traits on the other end of the spectrum. Of course, some scientists want to explain these traits in terms of molecules and physiology. But molecules don't covet, people do. External forces, perhaps whole tracts of thought, can put suggestions in the mind in the same form of our own consciousness. They seem to work in similar fashion in many people, as if they were coordinated.

"We do not easily discern these powers. They seem like our everyday part of living, and in fact are. As humans, we have continual needs, and our extra desires don't always feel that much different. We simply want something not necessary for biological survival. Materialism is only one example. Jealousy, easy anger, all these may be affected by forces."

Dana's face was a study of concentration.

Allen continued. "It seems like there are 'tracks' we get into that pull us into certain behaviors. You know how we may say someone is 'off track.' Specific behavior patterns could emerge from an existing situation, like the rationalizing a CEO does to increase his own income to ridiculous amounts, possible because of his very successful business. He gets onto a 'fast track' of production and accumulation of resources, and somehow he, or she, starts thinking in a certain way.

"Your 'tracks' remind me of Fuji's soul language. She says we live in some kind of geometrically-related existence which we don't sense in ordinary ways."

"When Christ talks about the 'straight and narrow,' I really believe he was referring to our inner selves being able to find this place and know it was what God wanted for his creation. If you created an earth and people, wouldn't you want some guidelines to keep it from chaos? People love games and learn and accept all kinds of rules for them, but they can't understand why there should be rules for what is much more than a game, life itself.

"God must have known that in His system of giving us thoughts, consciousness and free will, that there would be ways that consciousness could be twisted. After Adam's fall, the forces existed to do it. External thoughts could come into a mind and influence the thoughts generated by the individual. Behavior could be altered, and not for the better.

"God sent Christ to save us from the effects of the resulting sins. Jesus' own act had power in it. When our minds believe in Him, they are changed. And our souls are lifted, even through death."

Dana looked out the window to the artificially lit snow. "It's scary to deal with spiritual struggles. No matter what our IQ may be, we are all weak and susceptible spiritually. We are talking about forces which we may experience but really have little true understanding."

"I struggle with it, too. In one sense, I don't like to think about the supernatural. Aren't Christians supposed to be more concerned with being loving and kind than with the 'fantastic?' And yet what is prayer but the supernatural transfer of thoughts? When you believe in Christ, you need not fear."

Dana breathed deeply. It seemed each new situation she found herself in called for action in renewing her faith. She said, "You think 'Joe' is affected by a dark force?"

"I don't know. It's OK to be concerned about the government not being fair. But it's when you are under the influence of the devil that you start thinking about instigating violence. As they say, two wrongs do not make a right. The second just adds more hurt to the first."

The next morning, Dana walked dejectedly along one of LC's hallways. Would God involve them in the bomb situation, or was He asking them to pray and wait? Of course other individuals, such as the police, would be working on the case. But what about the motivations of the perpetrators? What was the key to their behavior?

Dana glanced at one of the bulletin boards. A colorful sheet announced a speaker, named Derrick Shipley, member of a local anti-landmine group, MINE BAN. He'd be coming to their auditorium February 2. Dana wrote the details in her notebook to report to FISH. She'd ask the group about talking with Shipley. Maybe he'd have ideas of who was placing the mines.

At home, she thought she'd see if Shipley was listed in the phone book so she'd have the info at the meeting. Her finger which found his name quivered when she realized his address was the one to which the skier had driven!

FISH next met on Saturday evening. Perry took advantage of the change in their regular schedule to combine their meeting with a catered dinner. The members came into his own home from a snowy evening, one of those where the scenery of evergreens with white boughs and willowy flakes flowing quickly to land made Dana giddy and optimistic. The others laughed as they arrived, shaking their coats and stomping boots. They sat around the dining table like a family at a holiday meal, and felt the bonds among themselves.

When the meal was done, and Perry closed the glass French door to the room to keep their discussion from the people cleaning up, he called them again to prayer. "Lord, we are here to see what has transpired among your servants. We thank you for your gracious ways and look forward to discovering your will. We pray for your help in this serious matter we find among our neighbors and ourselves."

Dana had urged Allen to share his concern about his friend, 'Joe.' When finished, he asked the others, "Do you think I should go north and seek him out? Talk with him?"

Eben said, "Maybe it's a good idea, since you keep thinking of him. If he isn't involved, he might know someone who is."

"I'd be concerned about that," Kathryn countered. "The love Allen showed this man may be keeping him straight. 'Joe' certainly must have heard about what's happened and I think he'd figure out what was on Allen's mind. That might be painful and deflating to him."

Some of the others nodded.

Kathryn continued. "You associated the man you know with the events of Dana's experience, but that doesn't mean that your suspicions are pure truth. We must always be careful of our imaginations. That's why we are here together--to help us sort our own thoughts to compare with what we believe is God's will and way.

"True," said Ranjah, "but we also believe God

communicates in unusual ways, and we have to be alert to them."

"And also alert to the false impressions the devil is able to devise," added Perry.   "You know we have disagreement here. Lord, we will wait and look to you for guidance."

Dana piped up.   "I'm bursting to tell you what I found. There's a lecture by an anti-mine activist at LC's, and the guy lives at the house I saw!"

"What?" Allen ejected.

"His name's Derrick Shipley. Anyone know him?"

Fuji said, "Yeah, I've seen him written up in the paper. His picture was there, so I've recognized him around town. I think he's an accountant or something like that, but he puts a lot of time into this mine group. If I remember correctly, he's been to countries which have had mines planted and still have many civilian injuries."

"Anyone else know anything about him?" Perry asked. Upon the lack of response, he asked, "Should we contact him or his group?"

Fuji said, "He might be investigating the mines on his own."

"Maybe we should infiltrate the meetings," Allen suggested, "or break into the house."

"What would an anti-mine group have to hide?" Dana asked him.

"What was that note for?" Allen seemed irritated.

"It could have been anything," Dana snapped back, but then relented. "I guess I must admit he might know something. Perhaps he wants to let the mines go off for a while to make a point."

"We could take that a step further and suspect that they are doing it themselves," Kathryn added.

They sat in silence, shocked by the thought but not willing to dismiss it.

Dana shook her head. "It's hard to believe anyone would be so blind to what they are doing. How can someone be so against mines that they mine someone?"

Kathryn, looking rueful, said, "It may be extreme, but I think we see examples in human nature all too often, even in some Christians. Not only in the cases where, say, abortion doctors are killed, but in more subtle ways. We are disgusted with what others are doing, so we use hurtful rhetoric. We think somehow our bluntness will get them to stop, but don't realize how it feeds our own hatred. Divisive language and action does little to convince them and it creates walls we unknowingly use to protect and elevate ourselves."

Dana replied, "I think you are right, but happily, many Christians *do* understand, and behave accordingly.

Ranjah had been perched back in his chair, eyes closed as if in a trance. He opened them and said, "God is revealing these things to us. Though it gets harder the more we learn, I think we still should wait on Him."

Dana responded, "Maybe He's shown us so we can do something about it."

"Maybe the note was about another group's plans," Fuji said.

Allen wanted action. "At the least we should have a stakeout at the house."

"It may be too late by the time we figure out their activities," Dana countered.

"They may have already planted other bombs," Eben added.

"I say we go in," Allen said.

"If you are caught," warned Eben, "you'll have to

dissociate yourself with FISH. Not to mention the personal affect it could have on your future career. Or for that matter, your life."

Allen's expression froze. He had not considered the risk of losing his place in FISH.

"It is risky, Allen. The building could be a clubhouse, so there may be more than the occupant coming and going." Perry said. "You'll have to make your own decision if we agree you should try. And you'll need help. Dana, you could take one of my digital cameras. We'll put it in the 'flash off' mode--someone might notice a flash and get suspicious. You'll be able to use the illuminated screen to see what you'll get, and the shutter can be timed.

"I'll have the police chief ready to see the computer's results if you get anything. Of course, this is also your choice."

Allen jumped in. "I've looked at the house. At night, I've seen who I take now to be Shipley leave and turn out the lights. The door to the back porch is a screen door and may not be locked. The porch hides the house door and when it's dark we may be able to open the lock or get through a house window that opens to the porch. In these old houses the windows are wood frame. I've been in some houses in this neighborhood. Few of the windows are barred, and some don't even have locks on them. I'll bring a knife in case we have to get the glass out of the frame. Some of the basement windows look loose, but we would be seen.

"We should be able to get onto the back porch from the alley at night. There aren't any big lights in the back from this house or the neighbors. The back yard is not fenced. More importantly, in Shipley's half-block I didn't see any barking dogs kept in back."

Perry was surprised at Allen's thoroughness. "Looks like you're still willing to take the chance."

"In this case, I think it's worth it."

"I'm with Allen," Dana said, "but I'm concerned about any judge's reaction to the way we get the evidence."

Fuji answered, "Even if it doesn't get through the court, if the group has bombs, they would be exposed through the media coverage and innocent people would probably be saved."

Eben nodded. "We'd like justice for the persons already affected, but can we justify waiting for more to be hurt or killed?"

"What do you think, Ranjah?" Perry asked.

"May our mission be cloaked in God's care."

Amen, all answered.

The next night, the couple parked around the corner from the house, near the alley they would use. They saw the lights in Shipley's house go out. Crouching and in dark clothes, they saw no other people.

"Here we go," Allen whispered. They walked up the back yard and stepped to the porch. Allen grasped the screen door and it indeed opened.

Slipping through the door, Dana was relieved to be hidden by the porch, but still felt her heart pounding so hard she wondered if she'd be able to handle the camera.

Allen tried to credit card the lock of the door, but it was the old-fashioned square type. He tried to shove a window open. "Dang," he said. "It's locked."

"I guess I'd lock it too if I stashed land mines here."

"The wood is rotted. There only two panes in the window. I'm going to take one out."

"If he comes home, he'll see."

"Let's hope that's after we leave. I'll put it right below the window. It might look like it came out on its own."

Allen peeled at the dried and broken calk.

"Don't let it crash," Dana warned.

"Thanks, I never thought of that."

"Sorry."

Dana didn't know whether to try to help or stay clear. Minutes seemed to fly by. Allen finally pulled the glass toward him and set it down. He pushed Dana through and she helped him in. Their eyes were already accustomed to the dark.

"Basement or second floor first?" Allen asked.

"I have a feeling about the upstairs."

They tip-toed through a living and dining area to a front foyer and stairwell.

They climbed and gingerly started checking rooms. Dana hoped none of Shipley's buddies had stayed behind. A bathroom, a bedroom. Then, a large room filled with olive-colored cases.

"I think we've got it!" Dana whisper-shrieked.

"We need more than boxes on your pictures," Allen said. He checked the cases and found with relief that they weren't locked. He pulled open the lid of one and knew they hit paydirt. He set a few mines in front of the cases.

Dana had already set up the camera. The bedroom window had torn curtains which were light-weight enough to allow a little light, but Dana had her doubts about enough illumination even with her small tripod. She tried to follow Perry's instructions for shutter time.

A car approached the house. The street was moderately traveled, but this one seemed to be slowing.

The seconds it took for exposure were almost more than she could bear.

"Want to take more?" Allen asked.

"Yes, but I want to get out of here even more. That car is parking out front." She gathered the camera equipment.

He put the mines back. "Let's go."

They crept downstairs. Through the window they saw the man with the hunting cap get out of his car. They ran to the kitchen as he came up to the porch, and pushed through the kitchen window as he turned the key in the lock and opened the front door. They ran through the back screen door and crouched through the back yard as light filtered through the house from the front rooms. They ran through the alley and then tried to look normal as Allen unlocked the car's doors. Once inside, Dana locked the doors as Allen started the engine. No one had followed them. As he pulled out, Dana said, "Thank you, thank you, Lord."

Allen took a deep breath. "If we had gone to the basement first, we wouldn't have had time."

The police chief was at Perry's home. He had already prepared a warrant for the clubhouse. He shook their hands and said, "Let's hope no one figures out you were there before we can get to them." Dana gave Perry the camera. She was almost as nervous now as she was taking the shots. She'd feel terrible if the pictures didn't show the mines.

Perry pulled up the pictures on his computer. The mines and cases showed so clearly they could read the serial numbers on the boxes. Perry said, "Good work.

They came through." Dana was thrilled.

Perry printed out the pictures while the chief phoned his units and ordered a raid. In a matter of minutes, the report came back to the chief. The mines were recovered and the man in the home arrested.

The next meeting took place at the FISH headquarters. Perry brought everyone up to date. "The prosecutor will not reveal our identity. There are precedents for anonymous sources of evidence in court cases. We hope our absence does not affect the case."

He added, "The guy in the hunting cap was one of Shipley's MINE BAN group, Dale Regent. He lives here in Lake City. We're glad for Allen's sake it wasn't his friend, 'Joe.' Regent is cooperating to help the police locate Shipley, who must have seen the police cars near the house, since he and others from the group haven't appeared. Regent told us they were planning to meet Jan. 29 at 8:00 pm to plant hundreds of mines within a few hundred square miles. They of course didn't want to spread the word by phone, so had elaborate systems of informing each other, hence the note in the tree.

"I believe God is just, even above and beyond our own legal systems. Whether Shipley lands in jail or not, he will pay in the life he leads. He will never have peace unless he gets right with God."

Allen said, "Now I'm glad I didn't visit 'Joe' when I had thought it might be him. But I do want to go up north to see him soon."

Perry said, "I'd like Dana to write up the mission for a report for us, and perhaps she can send it in to a Christian magazine, using our code names.

Dana instantly visualized a story: *The End of the World.* "You know, Perry, I would totally enjoy that." She added sheepishly, "That is, if the publishers would accept it."

Perry grinned. "We'll leave that up to God. We have confidence in your abilities. In fact, you might start writing about all our missions."

"This mission worked out from one point of view," said Eben. "The perpetrators were caught. But what about their state of mind? Has that changed?"

"What about the state of their soul?" Fuji asked.

Perry had lit the fireplace in a cozy den across the hall from the meeting room and invited the members to stay for awhile after the prayer was done. Kathryn, Dana and Allen moved there, but the others were still involved in their own conversations.

Allen and Dana sat back on one of the couches and looked into the fire.

"I'm going to move to a place in the country," said Allen.

"Won't you miss your derelicts?" said a surprised Dana.

"Maybe I'll go back to prison ministry for a while. You know, near the prison outside the city, where Shipley and his friends will probably go. I think people need to know how humans, if they hold on to lies, become twisted. And there's a way to know truth from falsehood."

"God's Word is the Truth."

"Jesus sets our lives straight if we put Him before politics, before our own fears, before ourselves."

Kathryn said, "You used the words, 'twisted' and

'straight.' I find myself thinking more and more about 'soul language.' The Bible makes many references to the *heart* which imply character and emotion. Words and their meanings are very deep-seated in consciousness, with a close connection to inner energy. I think the soul and body are interacting in ways which give us a sense of the Spirit of Truth. In the book Jeremiah, God says He will write the law into His peoples' hearts. Someday we will understand more fully.

Dana reflected, "The human soul can be enmeshed into various forces. God is trying to tell us how it works as plainly as He can without compromising the exciting and mysterious texture of the life He has given us."

Then Dana cocked her head and frowned. "Allen, if you move from Lake City, what about FISH?"

"We can drive in to FISH meetings."

"We?"

"Don't you think it's about time to plan the wedding?" Allen asked before planting a big fat kiss on Dana's cheek.

Dana smiled, supremely satisfied. "I've always wanted to live in the country."

The rest started to move in from the dining area. They sat quietly and comfortably, enjoying the glow of God's leadership through another mission.

Dana looked at Allen, and she felt her own heart, joyous for where it had led her. To Allen, to FISH, to her wonderful, lovely Savior.